A GUIDE TO THE NATIONAL LOTTERY

A PRACTICAL HANDBOOK FOR APPLICANTS

by

Howard Hurd

A DIRECTORY OF SOCIAL CHANGE PUBLICATION

A GUIDE TO THE NATIONAL LOTTERY
A practical handbook for applicants
By Howard Hurd

Published by
Directory of Social Change,
Radius Works, Back Lane,
London, NW3 1HL.

© 1995 Directory of Social Change

Designed and typeset by Kate Bass

Printed by Clifford Frost Limited

British Library Cataloguing-in-Publication Data
A catalogue record for this book is available from the British Library

ISBN 1 873860 67 6

DISCLAIMER
The information contained in this book is intended for guidance only, and was correct at the time of going to press. Before submitting any application for lottery funding you should carefully read all information supplied by the distributing body concerned and follow all instructions given.

CONTENTS

· ·

PART 1: INTRODUCTION

PART 2: THE DISTRIBUTING BODIES

PART 3: OTHER INFORMATION

Part 1:
INTRODUCTION

THE NATIONAL LOTTERY

The National Lottery is now well and truly upon us, and is on the way to becoming the world's largest state lottery. It has already created its first multi-millionaires, substantially benefited the government's coffers, and generated many millions of pounds which will eventually reach a range of good causes.

The main bulk of this book gives advice on how to make applications for money from the bodies responsible for distributing the proceeds of the National Lottery to the arts, sport, national heritage, charities, and projects to commemorate the turn of the millennium.

This introduction considers some of the broader issues, such as

- Why and how was the National Lottery set up?
- How much money does it generate and where does this money go?
- What are the wider implications of the National Lottery?

WHY A NATIONAL LOTTERY?

The historical background

The idea of a national lottery is neither new nor original. The first national lottery in Britain was run in 1569 to fund repairs to the Cinque Ports, and for the next 250 years state-sponsored lotteries were regularly held.

During the 17th century most of the lotteries were for specific purposes, usually to provide for exceptional items of public expenditure. They provided finance for Britain's plantations in Virginia (1612), funded repairs to our fishing fleet following damage inflicted by the Spaniards (1640), and even paid the ransom of English slaves held in Tunis (1660). In the 18th century, lottery proceeds were more likely to find their way into the exchequer to support general government expenditure. Occasionally they were still used to fund special projects such as the building of Westminster Bridge (1739) and the construction of what is now the British Museum (1753).

All this came to an end in 1826, however, when the government of the day stopped running state lotteries. This action was a response to problems which had become increasingly apparent, such as illegal betting on the lottery outcome and other 'social evils' which were thought to be the 'constant and fatal attendants' of lotteries.

For the best part of the next two centuries, national lotteries were not held, although their resurrection was considered at various times. The 1932-33 Royal Commission on Gambling examined the cases for and against the revival of large lotteries, but felt that the perceived side effects were still too great.

Three decades later, the re-introduction of a national lottery was the subject of a private member's bill which received a second reading in 1968, but a subsequent new clause to the 1968 Finance Bill was defeated on a free vote. During the debate, the Financial Secretary to the Treasury argued that part of the proceeds of any national lottery should go to desirable purposes or objects and some should be retained by the government for general revenue. The matter was subsequently re-considered by a working party set up by the Home Office which looked more widely at large scale lotteries for charities and sports. Its findings, reported in 1973, again threw out the concept of a national lottery.

More recent events

By the late 1970s the tide was beginning to turn. The first indication came from the 1978 Royal Commission on Gambling chaired by Lord Rothschild. It recommended that a single national lottery be set up to benefit sport, the arts and other deserving causes, with a 10 per cent tax revenue for the exchequer. The Royal Commission provided the following justification for its support:

'One of the most appealing features of an independently administered but state sponsored national lottery for good causes is that it escapes or by-passes the normal Government decision-making procedures for resource allocation. In practice, a Government of any party, subject to day to day public and political pressures, finds it impossible to devote more than meagre resources to good causes of the kind which are desirable rather than essential...There is a crucial need in our society for a source of substantial funds to provide support of a kind with which any Government experiences great difficulty.' (Cmnd 7200, 13.62-63).

Its recommendations were not, however, adopted by the government, and the idea of a national lottery was put on the back-burner for the ensuing decade before reappearing with fresh impetus in the 1990s.

Part of the momentum came from within the voluntary sector itself. In 1990 Ralf Dahrendorf, long time trustee of the Ford Foundation, wrote an article for the *Times* in which he argued for the creation of a major new foundation which could act as an independent source of reform. He suggested a national lottery as a possible source of funding for such a body, although he also put forward two other alternatives: the proceeds of the privatisation of public assets or massive gifts from wealthy individuals.

The fundamental reason for the resurrection of the national lottery idea was, however, that once again its political time had come, fitting neatly in with the Thatcherite (and post-Thatcherite) notions of self-help and voluntary provision. In 1991 a private member's bill was introduced by Ivan Lawrence MP which proposed the creation of a national lottery to benefit the arts, sports and heritage, with charities added as a fourth residual beneficiary after lobbying by the National Council for Voluntary Organisations (NCVO) amongst others.

Although the bill was defeated at the second reading in January 1992, within two months the government produced a White Paper entitled *A National Lottery: Raising Money for Good Causes*. As the title suggests, the main justification put forward in the White Paper for a national lottery revival was the money it would provide for a range of good causes – arts, sports, heritage and charities.

The Conservative Party's manifesto for the 1992 election, released shortly after the White Paper, promised that a national lottery would be set up if they regained power. They proposed that the lottery should benefit five good causes – the four mentioned in

3

the White Paper and a new addition, the Millennium Fund, to support projects celebrating the transition from one millennium to another at the end of this century.

These proposals were presented as an indication of the Tories' commitment to arts, culture and the heritage. But an income-tax reducing Conservative government no doubt saw a national lottery as a form of voluntary taxation imposed on a 'pay-as-you-play' basis – part of the proceeds going directly into the exchequer – with a significant feel good factor thanks to the benefits to good causes. The Conservatives must also have been influenced by the fruits of national lotteries run in various countries around the world (see below), and hoped that their success could be replicated in the UK. Whatever the motivation, upon their return to power these election promises became reality with the introduction of the *National Lottery etc Act* a year later.

The experience of other countries

The first recorded public lottery took place nearly 2 millennia ago when a lottery was held in 10 A.D. to finance repairs of ancient Rome. Italy also appears to have been the starting point of the wave of lotteries financing great public projects which spread across medieval Europe. One of these early lotteries, Holland's *klassenlotterie* game which was developed around 1600, is still going strong.

The spread of lotteries around the world continued over successive centuries, but there has been a recent flurry of activity. In 1993 there were over 150 state sponsored lotteries held around the world, with total sales estimated at nearly £53 billion. Every country in Europe now has a lottery, and they are also held by countries including the US, Canada, Brazil, Australia, New Zealand, Japan, Israel, and the former Soviet Union.

In most cases, once prizes have been paid the money is either added to general state revenues (as is the case in France and Sweden) or is put towards specific public or semi-public causes (such as Sydney Opera House, which was funded by the New South Wales State Lottery). It is relatively rare that part of lottery proceeds are distributed to the voluntary sector, although this does happen in the Netherlands, Belgium, and most German states.

HOW THE NATIONAL LOTTERY WAS SET UP

National Lottery etc Act 1993

The *National Lottery etc Act 1993* put in place the necessary structures for the creation of a new national lottery in the UK.

Part I of the Act determined that the National Lottery is to be regulated by the Director General of the National Lottery, an individual appointed for a five year term by the Secretary of State for National Heritage. The Director General heads OFLOT, the Office of the National Lottery, the main regulatory body. The Director General is also responsible for awarding the operating licence to run the National Lottery to the private sector. The Secretary of State can, however, impose any requirements or restrictions he/she considers necessary, especially with regard to the minimum age at which tickets can be purchased (16 years at present), the use of the National Lottery logo or signage, and the type of information presented in lottery advertisements.

Part II of the Act deals with the distribution of the proceeds of the National Lottery. It specifies that the share of the lottery turnover to benefit good causes be paid by the lottery operator into the National Lottery Distribution Fund, controlled and managed by the Secretary of State. The money will then be divided by the National Lottery Distribution Fund between five areas of expenditure:

- arts
- sport
- national heritage
- charities
- projects to mark the year 2000 and start of the new millennium

The Act determined that each of these five good causes would initially receive 20 per cent of the available money, although the Secretary of State has the power to vary these proportions above a 5 per cent minimum. After December 31st 2000 (if the date is not made any later by the Secretary of State), projects to mark the millennium will receive no further finances from the National Lottery Distribution Fund, and the remaining four good causes will receive a correspondingly higher proportion.

The Act appoints the following organisations as distributing bodies for the five good causes:

i. Arts

The portion of the National Lottery proceeds to benefit the arts will be distributed by the four Arts Councils. The Act specifies that the Arts Council of Great Britain should receive 97.2 per cent of the arts money to allocate to projects in England, Scotland and Wales, and the Arts Council of Northern Ireland should get the remaining 2.8 per cent. The Arts Council of Great Britain has subsequently split into separate national councils, so that the arts funds are now allocated according to relative population levels along the following lines:

- Arts Council of England   83.3%
- Scottish Arts Council   8.9%
- Arts Council of Wales   3.0%
- Arts Council of Northern Ireland   2.8%

ii. Sport

The four national Sports Councils are given responsibility for distributing lottery funding for sport. Like the money for the arts, it is split amongst the four national councils according to relative population levels:

- Sports Council (England)   83.3%
- Scottish Sports Council   8.9%
- Sports Council for Wales   3.0%
- Sports Council for Northern Ireland   2.8%

iii. National Heritage

The lottery proceeds allocated for expenditure on the national heritage are to be distributed for the whole of the UK by the trustees of the National Heritage Memorial Fund, a pre-existing body. The National Lottery Act amends the National Heritage Act 1980, which created the National Heritage Memorial Fund, so that its trustees have greater grant-making powers in connection with lottery monies. They can use lottery proceeds to fund the construction, acquisition, improvement or conversion of any building designed to house objects of importance to the national heritage, and they can also help provide visitor facilities aimed at promoting public enjoyment and knowledge of our heritage.

iv. Charities

The National Lottery Charities Board, a new body set up in the Act, is given the responsibility of using its share of lottery funds to support both:

- charities *per se,* and
- institutions, other than charities, that have been established for charitable purposes (whether or not they are charitable in the eyes of the law), benevolent purposes or philanthropic purposes.

The Act specifies that the National Lottery Charities Board is to consist of a chair along with 16 other members, all appointed by the Secretary of State (who can also increase the number of members if he/she thinks it necessary). The allocation of money to England, Scotland, Wales and Northern Ireland is to be handled by four sub-committees of the Board (each consisting of a chair and at least two other members).

v. Millennium

The Millennium Commission, another new body set up in the Act, is given the task of handling the distribution of lottery funds towards projects to mark the change of millennium. The Act specifies that the Commission consists of nine members appointed by the Queen on the recommendation of the Prime Minister, two being Government ministers (one as chair) and one nominated by the Leader of Opposition. After December 31st 2000 the Secretary of State can reduce the number of Commissioners to three.

The Secretary of State has the power to issue directions to the distributing bodies about the recipients, purposes, and conditions of the grants they make (directions were subsequently presented in June 1994, and are summarised on p.17). The Act excludes distributing bodies from giving money to:

- any organisation of which the distributing body is a member;
- any organisation over which the distributing body has control or material influence;
- any organisation the Secretary of State believes is concerned with terrorism in Northern Ireland, or which promotes or encourages terrorism.

The remainder of the National Lottery Act does not deal directly with the National Lottery, but aims to take account of some of its potential effects on other lotteries and the football pools. Part III of the Act makes changes to the regulations regarding small lotteries, such as those run by many voluntary groups, so that they are easier to hold (advertising rules are relaxed and registration simplified) and more attractive to enter (the maximum prize limit is increased from £12,000 to £25,000, or 10% of turnover, whichever is larger; and maximum turnover is increased from £180,000 to £1m). Similarly, Part IV relaxes some of the rules relating to the football pools, so that coupons and stakes can be handled by retail premises (which had previously been barred), allowing prizes to be 'rolled over' if not won, and reducing the minimum age of participants from 18 to 16.

How the National Lottery is regulated

As noted above, the National Lottery is officially regulated by OFLOT – the Office of the National Lottery – a quango which is independent of Government but answerable to parliament. The Director General of the National Lottery, currently Peter Davis, has a legal responsibility under the National Lottery etc Act 1993 to ensure that:

- the National Lottery is run 'with all due propriety',
- the interests of every participant in the National Lottery are protected,
- and, as long as the first two conditions are met, that the maximum amount possible is raised for the five good causes.

The Director General of the National Lottery is also responsible for selecting the company to run the National Lottery, with the main criteria being security and propriety, along with the largest expected return for good causes. OFLOT's address is: 2-4 Cockspur Street, London, SW1Y 5DH, Tel: 0345-125596.

Who runs the National Lottery?

In May 1994 the Director General chose Camelot Group plc out of the eight companies which had submitted a bid for the licence to operate the National Lottery for the first seven years (after this period there will be another tendering process). Camelot Group plc is entirely owned by five other firms:

- Cadbury Schweppes plc: the well-known sweets and drinks company, with experience in handling the retail outlets selling lottery tickets (22.5 per cent stake).
- De La Rue plc: a leading provider of high security printing and other security systems which help prevent fraud (22.5 per cent stake).
- GTECH UK Ltd: subsidiary of GTECH Corp, which operates lotteries in five continents around the world (22.5 per cent stake).
- Racal Electronics plc: specialist in the electronic communications needed to link lottery terminals (22.5 per cent stake).
- ICL plc: the computer firm, which provides the lottery terminals (10 per cent stake).

The total shareholding adds up to £50 million of funding. If their estimates are accurate, Camelot will eventually receive around £275m each year to cover their operating costs and provide their profits. Camelot's National Lottery Line telephone number is 01645-100000

HOW DOES THE NATIONAL LOTTERY WORK?

The National Lottery got under way on November 14th 1994 when the first tickets were sold for the *computerised on-line National Lottery game* in around 10,000 retail outlets around the UK. Although it is likely that you will already have taken part in the National Lottery, it is worth going over the main features.

The basis of the computerised National Lottery game is that you select six different numbers between 1 and 49 to go into the weekly draw. You mark your choices on a playslip, which you give to the retailer along with £1 for every set of six numbers you have chosen. The retailer enters your numbers into the Lottery computer terminal, and gives you a National Lottery ticket – a computer print-out confirming your numbers and the draw date. This National Lottery ticket is vital as your proof of entry, and if you lose it you will be unable to claim any prize you might win.

Every Saturday evening at around 8 pm the winning numbers are selected at random, on a live BBC1 television show, and then announced on various other media. Six main winning numbers are drawn along with a seventh bonus number. You win the jackpot (or a share of the jackpot) if your six numbers match all six of the main winning numbers that are drawn. If the main jackpot is not won, it can be 'rolled over' and added to the next week's prize for up to four consecutive weeks. You win the second largest prize if your selection includes five of the main numbers along with the bonus number. Otherwise you win a prize if your six numbers match three or more of the main winning numbers.

Apart from the lowest prize, which is fixed at £10 if you match three winning numbers, all of the prizes are variable depending upon the number of National Lottery tickets sold in that week and the number of people matching the same quantity of numbers as you. As you can choose any six numbers between 1 and 49, your numbers might be the same as those selected by other people who have entered the National Lottery that week. If this proves to be the case, and you win one of the larger prizes, it will be split amongst all those with the same winning numbers.

From Spring 1995 you should also be able to buy instant *win scratch cards* as part of the National Lottery. These will be available from the same retailers as the computerised lottery tickets. There will be a range of National Lottery instant win games available at any one time. Some games will give you a relatively good chance of winning one of a large number of small prizes, with a typical range of £10 to £10,000. Other instant-win games will have fewer, larger prizes, but a lower chance of winning. The odds of winning a prize in any of the instant win games will vary between 1 in 4 and 1 in 7.

A TYPICAL WEEK'S NATIONAL LOTTERY PAYOUT

*National Lottery prizes
for the draw on December 17th 1994*

Winning numbers: 3,5,9,13,14,38 **Bonus number:** 30

Winning selections	Number of winners	Prize	Odds of winning
JACKPOT 6 main numbers matched	2	£3,403,310 each	1 in 13,983,816
5 main numbers plus bonus number	14	£149,596 each	1 in 2,330,636
5 main numbers	831	£1,575 each	1 in 55,492
4 main numbers	60,325	£47 each	1 in 1,033
3 main numbers	1,151,351	£10 each (fixed)	1 in 57
TOTAL PAYOUT	1,212,523	£24,558,574	1 in 54

WHERE DOES THE NATIONAL LOTTERY MONEY GO?

The National Lottery is now one of the largest single consumer products in the UK, and weekly sales are currently running at around £50 million to £60 million each week, although sales tend to be higher when the jackpot has been 'rolled over' from the previous week. From time-to-time Camelot is using reserves to top up the jackpot to a guaranteed £10 million for a 'super draw', which also leads to an increase in sales.

On these initial figures, total National Lottery sales in the first year should be pretty close to the £2.7 billion Camelot estimated before the lottery started. Camelot also predicts that within a few years lottery sales should peak at about double this amount – £5.5 billion – with 27,000 ticket retailers and revenue boosted by the earnings from the instant win games. Over the course of the full seven years of its operating licence, Camelot predicts that total National Lottery sales will amount to £32 billion.

This is, by any measure, a massive amount of money – but where does it all go? The way in which Camelot anticipates the lottery takings will be split over the full seven years of its operating licence is shown in the chart below, alongside the amounts involved if the first year's estimated takings are divided in the same way.

Half of the amount raised from lottery sales (£1.35 billion in the first year) is returned to the general public as prizes, and the government levies a 12% tax on total sales, which goes straight to the treasury (£325 million). Camelot receives 5% (£135 million in the first year) to provide profits after covering operating costs such as expenditure on marketing, communications, field service and overheads. At present, there are no signs that Camelot intends to make any charitable donations directly from its own profits (as do most other large public companies), although it is looking at this possibility and reviewing its overall strategy for charitable support. The retailers who sell National Lottery tickets also receive a 5% commission on sales (£135m in total).

The remaining proceeds, just over one-quarter of lottery takings (around £750 million in the first year), are paid to the National Lottery Distribution Fund to be put towards arts, sport, heritage, charities, and the Millennium Commission. Each of the five good causes should receive around £150 million in the first year, which for arts and the sports will be split between the nations according to population levels: England 83.3% (£125m), Scotland 8.9% (£13.35m), Wales 5% (£7.5m), and Northern Ireland 2.8% (£4.2m).

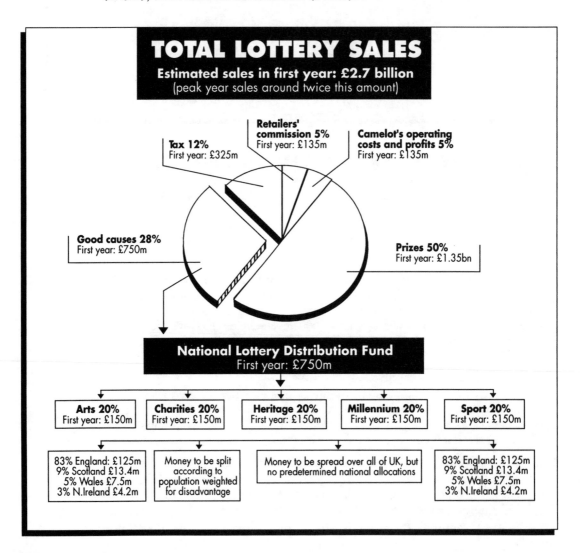

TOTAL LOTTERY SALES

Estimated sales in first year: £2.7 billion
(peak year sales around twice this amount)

Tax 12%
First year: £325m

Retailers' commission 5%
First year: £135m

Camelot's operating costs and profits 5%
First year: £135m

Good causes 28%
First year: £750m

Prizes 50%
First year: £1.35bn

National Lottery Distribution Fund
First year: £750m

Arts 20% First year: £150m	**Charities 20%** First year: £150m	**Heritage 20%** First year: £150m	**Millennium 20%** First year: £150m	**Sport 20%** First year: £150m
83% England: £125m 9% Scotland £13.4m 5% Wales £7.5m 3% N.Ireland £4.2m	Money to be split according to population weighted for disadvantage	Money to be spread over all of UK, but no predetermined national allocations		83% England: £125m 9% Scotland £13.4m 5% Wales £7.5m 3% N.Ireland £4.2m

WHAT ARE THE WIDER IMPLICATIONS OF THE NATIONAL LOTTERY?

Before the National Lottery was reintroduced, various concerns were raised about its wider implications. Although it is still too early to be able to determine with any certainty whether these fears were unfounded, the Lottery may have a number of significant side-effects.

Reductions in statutory funding

One of the main concerns about the Lottery is that it may provide an opportunity for the government to reduce its grant funding of bodies such as the Arts and Sports Councils. The government is, of course, quick to deny these charges, and has made it clear that it does not intend that the proceeds of the National Lottery will be used to replace statutory expenditure. The National Lottery White Paper gave the official position:

'The Government does not intend that the money provided from the lottery should substitute for that provided in other ways: the proceeds will not be brought within the planning total, and the Government will not make any case by case reduction in conventional expenditure programmes to take account of awards from the lottery proceeds.' (Cmnd1816, para7).

Whether or not this proves to be the case will become apparent when the government announces the level of its support for the Arts and Sports Council now the Lottery takings have reached the distributing bodies.

Reductions in public donations to charities

Another major concern is the effect the National Lottery may have upon the level of support charities receive from the general public, whose generosity has already been squeezed by the recession. The lottery has been marketed, in part, on grounds of the benefits it will bring to a range of good causes. Shortly before the first tickets were sold, double-page advertisements from Camelot appeared in the national press telling us that: 'Every time you play the National Lottery, someone else gets a better chance'. Rather than giving their money directly to charities, people may choose to buy a ticket for the National Lottery, which gives them a chance of winning a fortune as well as benefiting good causes.

Ian Ventham, head of fundraising at the Royal National Lifeboat Institution, expresses the fears of many within the charitable sector: 'There are two problems as I see it. The amount of cash put in collecting boxes will be less because of the disposable income spent on the lottery. And secondly the government has promoted the lottery so people think it is in aid of good causes.'

Whilst charities are receiving a share of the proceeds from the National Lottery, along with the four other good causes, this will only amount to around £150 million in the first year, rising to about twice this level in peak years. Research by the NCVO suggests, however, that reductions in spontaneous charitable gifts caused by the lottery will more than offset any new money for charities. Stuart Etherington, director of the NCVO, comments that: 'Charities will lose up to £36 million a year. While we support the lottery as a way of getting additional money for charities, it seems that 5 per cent of those polled said they would either reduce or replace their individual donations as a result.'

It is still too early to say for sure whether this rather gloomy prediction has become reality, and the NCVO is undertaking an on-going programme of research to keep track of the situation. It is instructive, however, to look at the experience of the voluntary sector in the Republic of Ireland following the start of the Irish National Lottery for good causes eight years ago. A survey of 100 Irish charities found that one third had suffered a decrease in their fundraising income since the lottery had started, and that although many had received lottery grants, the overall view was that the lottery had a negative effect upon voluntary giving in Ireland.

Impact on smaller lotteries

Research commissioned by the Arts and Sports Councils before the lottery got under way suggested that 4 per cent of the expenditure on charity raffle or lottery tickets by the general public would be diverted to the National Lottery. Despite the various measures introduced in the National Lottery Act to improve the pulling-power of smaller lotteries and raffles run by voluntary organisations, the lottery already seems to have had an adverse effect.

Contributions to Arthritis Care's 1994 Christmas Draw reportedly fell by £10,000 to £80,000 following several years of steady increase – its fundraising director Peter Maple placed part of the blame on the National Lottery. Tenovus, the leading Welsh cancer care and research charity, has similarly found that its own scratchcard lottery game cannot compete against the huge prizes offered by the National Lottery, and has had to cut the number of supermarket outlets selling its scratchcards from 150 to 90.

Again, the Irish experience does not offer much cause for optimism. In the first three years after the start of the Irish lottery, charities lost around 60 per cent of their income from small lotteries, and many have subsequently been shut down. There has been some attempt to fight back, however, by some of the smaller lotteries such as Rehab Lotteries, who launched a campaign with the punchline: 'Play the National Lottery and who loses?'. The negative impact of the National Lottery upon small charity lotteries in the UK can only worsen, however, when National Lottery scratchcard games are introduced in Spring 1995.

Effect on football pools and betting shops

It is not only the voluntary sector which is feeling the pinch because of the National Lottery – it is also having an adverse impact upon the betting industry. The director general of the Betting Office Licensing Association, Tom Kelly, has said that the turnover of Britain's betting shops may fall by up to 5 per cent because of the National Lottery, with a consequent 25 per cent reduction in profits. Research conducted before the lottery started for the Levy Board suggested that the bulk of bookies' customers expected to buy lottery tickets.

The story is the same for the football pools companies. Weekly pools takings are reportedly down by 17 per cent, and spot-the-ball turnover has been cut by one-quarter. Their main complaint in public, however, is what they see as the unfair advantage held by the National Lottery which is allowed to advertise on television and radio, whereas the pools companies are not, and it is also obliged to allocate a lower proportion of its takings to tax (12 per cent) and to good causes (28 per cent). The football pools are taxed much more heavily (37.5 per cent goes in betting duty), and pay 5 per cent plus a further 5p in every £1.05 to good causes (in particular sport and the arts).

More worrying for the non-profit sector, however, are the possible implications for the future of the Foundation for Sport and the Arts, which is funded by pools takings from Littlewoods, Vernons and Zetters. The fear must be that if football pools' takings continue to suffer at the hands of the National Lottery then the contribution may be curtailed. Recent press reports indicate that the weekly revenue paid by the pools companies to the foundation has indeed fallen from £1.4 million to £500,000. This is particularly ironic as the Sports and Arts Councils are suggesting that organisations after small amounts (less than £5,000 or £10,000) who are not normally eligible to apply for lottery funds should instead approach the Foundation for Sport and the Arts.

The Football Trust, which gives grants to help improve football stadia, has also reportedly seen its weekly income from the pools companies drop from £700,000 to only £160,000, the sharper decline in funding due to its greater dependence upon spot-the-ball takings.

Regressive effect

One of the major concerns about the National Lottery is that it is a regressive form of taxation. The experience of lotteries in other countries and research undertaken in this country prior to the start of the lottery indicate that poorer social groups are more likely to participate than better-off social groups. They also tend to devote a higher proportion of their income to gambling on lotteries.

Whilst this trend is worrying in itself, the regressive effect of the National Lottery is compounded by the nature of the activities which will receive much of the money for good causes, as it is the more affluent social groups who tend to make the greatest use of arts, sports and heritage facilities. The net effect of the National Lottery may be that income is transferred from lower income groups towards facilities from which the higher income groups receive the greatest benefit. This potentially redistributive effect was noted by the Association of Charitable Foundations' report on the lottery, *A Chance for Charities?*, which commented that: 'it is clear that the national lottery as a whole could be criticised, with some justification, for taking money from the poor in order to spend it on the rich.'

HOW DO YOU APPLY FOR MONEY FROM THE NATIONAL LOTTERY?

Read on...

Part 2:

THE DISTRIBUTING BODIES

GENERAL PRIORITIES

On January 4th 1995 most of the lottery distributing bodies opened their doors to applications. By the end of that first day they had received requests for grants totalling more than £1 billion, even though only £750m for good causes is expected from the lottery in its initial year. The competition for funds is clearly intense and you will only stand a chance of success if your project is eligible for funding. The following sections on each of the distributing bodies will help you decide whether you should apply for a grant from the lottery proceeds.

Whilst there are variations between the different distributing bodies, there are some general similarities in overall policies, especially between those handling the arts, sport and heritage funds. These overall priorities are based on policy directions issued in June 1994 by Peter Brooke, who was then Secretary of State for National Heritage, in order to guide the grant-making policies of the bodies responsible for allocating lottery funding (see box on opposite page).

These directions have been used by the distributing bodies as the basis of their grant-making criteria. As a result, there are some broad similarities in the types of organisations and projects that the sports, arts, heritage and Millennium bodies will consider for funding. In most cases, eligible bodies include charities and other voluntary organisations, local authorities and other public sector bodies, and educational establishments such as schools, colleges and universities. Some will also provide funding for projects run by private companies, but only if these projects are for the public benefit and not private gain. In all cases, individuals are excluded from applying for funds on their own behalf.

As for the types of projects which are eligible, with the exception of the National Lottery Charities Board there is an overall preference for projects involving capital expenditure, which have obtained partnership funding from non-lottery sources, and which are above a minimum cut-off size (which varies between £2,000, £5,000 and £10,000, but may be as low as £200 for the Charities Board). All of the distributing bodies require a high degree of accessibility to the general public, implementation of equal opportunity policies and a full consideration of access for people with a disability (see Appendix II for guidance).

There are variations in the details of the application process between the different distributors, which are considered in turn in the following sections. The information contained in this book is intended for guidance only, and was correct at the time of going to press. Before submitting any application you should carefully read all information supplied by the distributing body concerned and follow all instructions given. All of the distributors require an application form to be completed, although for some you first have to give advance notice of your intentions. The length of the application form also varies, as does the amount of supporting documentation you are required to submit, but in all cases the information required centres around your organisation and your proposed project.

The information provided in Part 3 of this book should help with various aspects of the application process. There are brief guidelines on project development, providing

POLICY DIRECTIONS ISSUED BY THE SECRETARY OF STATE FOR NATIONAL HERITAGE

The bodies responsible for distributing the National Lottery proceeds to good causes should take the following matters into account:

1 They should not solicit particular applications from particular organisations.

2 They must consider applications relating to the complete range of activities falling within their particular remit. *[This does not apply to the Millennium Commission.]*

3 They must ensure that money is only distributed to projects which are of benefit to the general public or which are charitable. Any project seeking funding must not have private gain as a primary purpose.

4 Funds should be concentrated on projects which involve *capital* expenditure on new and improved facilities. Money should only be used for *revenue* grants or for setting up endowments where these costs are connected with capital projects which have already received lottery funding and would not otherwise be completed because of a lack of other sources of finance. *[There are slightly different rules for the National Lottery Charities Board and the Millennium Commission, see below.]*

5 The viability of projects must be taken into account, and in particular there should be available resources to pay for future running and maintenance costs.

6 Projects must be supported by a significant element of partnership funding from non-lottery sources, which may include gifts in kind. *[This does not apply to the National Lottery Charities Board, see below.]*

7 Distributing bodies should obtain such information as they consider necessary to make decisions, and may wish to consult with independent expert advisers.

8 Distributors must not give money to any organisation over which they have material influence or control (this repeats a condition laid down in the National Lottery Act).

Distributing bodies should look for the highest standards of architectural quality and building design, with particular reference to general accessibility and the needs of people with disabilities.

The Secretary of State also issued the following directions to the separate distributing bodies:

Arts Councils

The four national Arts Councils must take account of the needs of projects involving film, the moving image and crafts.

National Heritage Memorial Fund

The National Heritage Memorial Fund trustees should aim to achieve an overall balance of funds for projects in each country in the UK according to relative population levels.

Millennium Commission

• The Millennium Commission must ensure that major projects are supported in every country of the UK.

• The Millennium Commission is permitted to support millennium celebrations and distribute money for bursary or similar schemes, as well as making grants for capital projects. It can also make revenue grants and endowments to support previously funded capital projects.

National Lottery Charities Board

The National Lottery Charities Board does not have to concentrate its funding on capital projects, and does not have to request that applicants obtain partnership funding. It has received further directions on grant distribution from the Home Secretary.

access for people with disabilities, potential sources of partnership funding, and details of organisations who may be able to offer further advice. If you are planning a major capital project involving several million pounds of lottery funding, you should also be aware of the European Union procurement regulations (outlined in Appendix III). And if you are lucky enough to be awarded a lottery grant, there will be a number of conditions attached, which are summarised in Appendix V (for the arts, heritage, millennium and sports funds).

The distributing bodies for arts, heritage and sports have similar grant-making timetables. Applications can be submitted on an on-going basis from January 4th 1995, with the first lottery funded grants likely to be awarded in Spring this year. The Millennium Commission has decided to hold annual competitions for grants: applications for the 1995 round have to be submitted by the end of April and the first grants will be announced in September. The National Lottery Charities Board is lagging behind most of the other distributors, and was still undertaking a consultation process at the start of 1995. It is likely to be in a position to accept applications sometime after the summer, and announce its first grants nearer the end of the year.

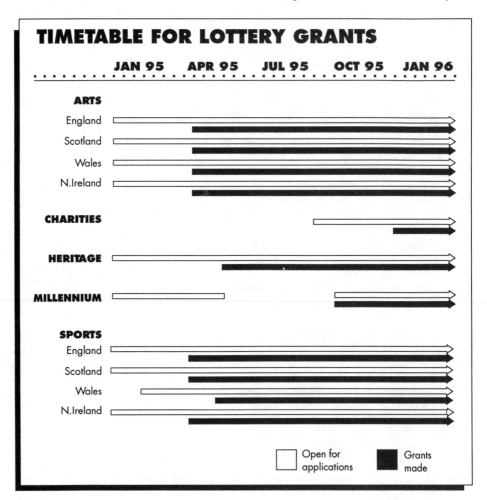

TIMETABLE FOR LOTTERY GRANTS

| | JAN 95 | APR 95 | JUL 95 | OCT 95 | JAN 96 |

ARTS
England
Scotland
Wales
N.Ireland

CHARITIES

HERITAGE

MILLENNIUM

SPORTS
England
Scotland
Wales
N.Ireland

☐ Open for applications   ■ Grants made

ARTS

STRUCTURE

The Distributing Bodies for the arts portion of the National Lottery takings are the *Arts Councils of England, Scotland, Wales and Northern Ireland.* The total budget for the arts is split amongst the four national Arts Councils in the following way:

- Arts Council of England   83.3%
- Scottish Arts Council   8.9%
- Arts Council of Wales   5.0%
- Arts Council of Northern Ireland 2.8%

These proportions were determined by the Secretary of State in the National Lottery etc Act 1993, and are based on the relative share of the UK population in each nation. The funds available in England are thus considerably greater than in the other regions: English projects will receive more than £80 million out of every £100 million generated by the National Lottery for the arts.

The arts councils of England, Scotland, Wales & Northern Ireland

Funding for capital projects in the arts

Minimum grant size normally considered:
- £5,000 (England)
- £5,000 (Scotland)
- £2,000 (Wales)
- £2,000 (Northern Ireland)

Opening date for applications:
- January 4th 1995 (England)
- January 4th 1995 (Scotland)
- January 4th 1995 (Wales)
- January 4th 1995 (Northern Ireland)

First grants announced:
- March/April 1995 (England)
- March 1995 (Scotland)
- April 1995 (Wales)
- Spring 1995 (Northern Ireland)

ENGLAND

The Arts Council of England (ACE) is responsible for allocating the share of the National Lottery proceeds to arts projects in England. The main locus for decisions is its National Lottery Board, an advisory committee of the Arts Council which has the power to make recommendations to it. The chair of the Board is Peter Gummer (brother of Tory government minister John Selwyn Gummer), and the other members are: Jon Foulds (chair of the Halifax Building Society), Patricia Hopkins (a renowned architect), Cleo Laine (jazz singer), Ruth Mackenzie (executive director of Nottingham Playhouse), Paddy Masefield (member of the National Disability Arts Forum and vice-chair of the Arts Council of England's arts and disability monitoring committee), Tony Pender (vice-chair of the Northern Arts Board, and an architect), Nima Poovaya-Smith (keeper of arts at Bradford Art Galleries and Museums), and David Puttnam (film producer and chair of the National Film and Television School). The board is serviced by the staff of the National Lottery Department at the Arts Council of England, which is headed by its director, Jeremy Newton.

ELIGIBLE BODIES

Bodies eligible for lottery funding from the Arts Council of England are: registered charities, non-profit distributing organisations, local authorities, schools, colleges, universities, amateur or voluntary groups, and public sector agencies. Commercial, or for-profit, organisations may also be eligible if they are able to show that their proposals will greatly benefit the public (and if such projects make a profit, the organisation may have to give part of it to the Arts Council). Eligible bodies will normally be based in England.

EXCLUDED BODIES

Individuals are not allowed to apply on their own behalf for lottery funds from the Arts Council of England. Neither are commercial organisations, unless the project is primarily for the benefit of the public rather than their own commercial interests.

ELIGIBLE PROJECTS

Projects eligible for funding from the ACE Lottery Board are capital projects in the arts taking place in England. The Arts Council includes the following amongst its definition of 'capital projects': constructing new buildings, improving old buildings, commissioning public works of art, and purchasing equipment, instruments or vehicles. Also included are the costs of carrying out the early development stages of a larger project by undertaking feasibility studies, briefing and design competitions.

All forms of the arts will be covered, including architecture, circus, crafts, dance, drama, film, the moving image, literature, mime, music, photography, video and the visual arts. During the first year of lottery funding the production of films or videos will also be eligible on a pilot basis (for which there are separate guidelines and application forms available from the Arts Council of England).

The ACE National Lottery Board will base its decisions on the following criteria, all of which it states are 'equally important':

Minimum grant size: £5,000

Whilst stating that projects of all sizes will be considered, the Arts Council National Lottery Board will not normally give grants of less than £5,000. It suggests that if you want to carry out small-scale building work or purchase small items of equipment you should either apply to other sources of grants (as detailed in its publication *Capital Grants for the Arts*), or you should co-operate with other grant-seeking organisations in your area and put forward a joint proposal for the development of larger-scale shared facilities.

Capital projects

As detailed above, only capital projects will be funded (in line with the Government's policy directions).

Public benefit

Priority will be given to projects which will have the widest possible impact by improving artistic facilities for the public or for artists and others who work in the arts. If your organisation has a restricted membership, or if it is a place of education, you must be able to show that the public will have access to the project for a substantial part of the time. Full consideration must also be given to the needs of people with disabilities, be they attending, performing, participating or working.

With this in mind, you will need to explain your plans to promote your work and your project to as many people as possible, through education and marketing to increase the potential audience's understanding and enjoyment.

Long-term viability

Any proposed project should have a clear and comprehensive management plan, controlled by a named manager, which includes budgets and timetables. You should also take into account the effect that any lottery-funding might have upon your organisation's future finances, as priority will given to those projects having a positive effect upon the long-term financial stability of the applicant.

Partnership funding

The Arts Council will not use lottery funds to fund the total cost of any proposed project. Instead it insists that you obtain partnership funding from other sources which cannot include non-lottery Arts Council budgets or other National Lottery distributors. The National Lottery Board will fund up to 90 per cent of projects costing less than £100,000, and up to 75 per cent of projects costing above £100,000.

This partnership funding can consist of financial contributions, support in-kind, or an agreement to support future project running-costs. It can also include any money raised for a particular project within the last three years.

Design and construction quality

There will be a preference for those showing the highest standards of architectural quality and building design. The Arts Council enforces this preference by stating that for large projects (costing over £100,000) it will give *priority* to those based on a successful feasibility study and suitable design competition. And if the project has a total cost of more that £1 million you are *expected* to proceed in this way, or they will want to know why not (unless important design decisions had been made before November 1994 when their guidelines were published). There is, however, a carrot attached to this stick, as the Arts Council has included feasibility studies, design competitions and the other early costs of project development as eligible 'capital projects' for lottery-funding. If you receive a grant for these purposes, it will not reduce your chance of future funding.

Quality of planned artistic activities & relevance to other plans

Applicants need to show how any proposed project will enhance the quantity and quality of their future artistic activities. The project should also be relevant

ARTS

to, and supported by, any other plans to develop the arts reflected in the policies and priorities of the Arts Council of England, Regional Arts Boards and individual local authorities, and should fit into the appropriate local, regional or national frameworks for arts planning.

Contribution of artists

Priority will be given to projects which result in the creation of new work and employment in the arts. Artists, craftspeople, and film and video makers should be utilised in the project work – they should be consulted about planning and design, employed as part of the design and construction team, or commissioned to create new work as part of a project or to commemorate the opening of new or improved facilities (these commissioning costs should be included in the total project costs).

EXCLUDED PROJECTS

Revenue funding

The Arts Council of England National Lottery Board will not normally give any money for day-to-day running costs or other revenue funding. The only circumstances in which it will consider requests for revenue or endowment funding are where the project has already received a lottery grant for capital expenditure.

Requests for grants of less than £5,000

The Arts Council will not normally use lottery funds to make grants of less than £5,000.

Projects outside England

The Arts Council only has powers to distribute lottery money to projects located in England. Arts projects in the other parts of the UK can apply for lottery funds from their relevant national Arts Council.

APPLICATIONS PROCEDURE

1. Obtain Application Pack

If you think you may be eligible for funding from the Arts Council of England's National Lottery Board, the first step is to obtain the application pack from the contact address below. You should then carefully check the eligibility criteria in the *Detailed Guidance to Applicants* booklet.

2. Complete and send *Advance Notice* at least 4 weeks before you want to submit your full application

If, having studied the eligibility criteria, you wish to apply for funds to support a capital arts project based in England, the next step is to fill in the *Advance Notice Form* contained in the application pack. This must be completed by all potential applicants. It asks for basic details concerning your organisation and your proposed project, including a brief project description, total project cost, amount requested from the Arts Council lottery funds, other lottery distributors, if any, who you will be approaching, and other sources of funding for the project. Once complete, the *Advance Notice* should be sent to the Arts Council of England Lottery Department at the address below.

3. Receive acknowledgement of *Advance Notice*

You will then receive a letter of acknowledgement from the Arts Council when it receives your *Advance Notice*. This letter will give you two important pieces of information: the lottery application number for your proposal, and the name of the lottery officer at the Arts Council Lottery Department who will be dealing with your application. If at any stage you have any queries about your application you should ask for this officer. The Arts Council started processing *Advance Notice* forms on December 1st 1994.

4. Complete and return application form
(at least four weeks after sending your *Advance Notice*)

You can then complete and send the full application form, but *at least four weeks* (and less than 12 months) must have elapsed since you submitted your *Advance Notice*. As it will be photocopied, you should fill the form out clearly using black ink or typed answers.

The application form is supplied by the Arts Council in their application pack, but you do not necessarily have to use this form. You can reproduce the form on your own word processor or computer, but only as long as you keep all the same questions in the same order as on the official application form. The Arts Council may also be able to supply a version of the application form on computer floppy disk (you should contact them on 0171-312 0123 if this would be useful).

Contents of application form

N.B. All questions should be answered, unless you are applying for funding for early development work in which case you may not know certain answers – if so you should write 'Not yet known' against them. Some answers may require more space than is available on the official application form – in these cases you should supply the information on separate sheets of paper attached to your form.

Details of your organisation

You will need to give details of your organisation, and the contact person responsible for the application. You have to specify the nature of your organisation, its age, and its aims and objective and state any previous or planned applications for lottery money from any of the distributing bodies.

Details of the project

You are required to give a brief description of the project (but you have to submit a full project description – see below), the estimated total project cost, and the amount you require from the Arts Council's lottery funds. A breakdown of the elements of this project cost and a timetable of the cashflow forecast also need to be supplied. Other project details required include: the type of art forms involved; how it fits into your organisation's

---

SUPPORTING DOCUMENTATION REQUIRED:

- Copy of Constitution or Memorandum and Articles of Association.
- Copy of latest audited accounts and budget for current financial year.
- A detailed and comprehensive project description.
- A copy of any relevant feasibility study, project design or brief.
- A full project budget, describing each item of income and expenditure in detail.
- Copy of project brief, if available.
- Financial projections for future years to show the long-term effects of the project.
- A copy of any relevant market research, education and audience development plan or commissioning plan which you have available.
- A detailed breakdown of the other sources of funding for the project, with an indication of whether these funds are committed, intimated, possible, or yet to be applied for.

Other information required for applications greater than £100,000:

- A detailed business plan for your organisation, starting in the next financial year and ending at least three years after the end of the project.
- A detailed cashflow forecast.

---

general aims; start and finish dates; project location; and preparations undertaken.

The benefits of the project

In this section you will need to give an indication of the beneficiaries of the project and how they will benefit, the impact of the project upon future artistic activity, its relation to local authority plans to develop the arts, how the project will reach the widest possible audience, and the ways in which the needs of people with disabilities will be addressed. Details are also requested on project management (both during and after completion), other sources of project funding, and how running costs will be met.

Building projects

If your project involves the construction of a new building or major changes to an existing structure, you should also complete the *Supplementary Application Form – Buildings* enclosed in your application pack. This asks a number of questions about your proposed building project, such as: the project manager and his/her level of previous relevant management experience; the ways in which bodies responsible for architecture or design have been chosen; whether planning permissions are needed or have been granted; and steps taken to ensure building quality and disability access.

Projects over £100,000

As detailed above, projects requiring more than £100,000 of lottery funding from the Arts Council of England are required to provide a detailed cashflow forecast and a detailed business plan.

You should then list (in the space provided) all the documents you are enclosing with your application, and then sign the standard declaration along with a member of your board. You should note that the Arts Council states that it is unable to return anything you may send it to support your application.

Once you have completed the application form you should send it, along with *Supplementary Application Form – Buildings* (if applicable), and one copy of all appropriate supporting documentation, to your named lottery officer at the address shown at the end of this section.

If you have any queries about the application form, or want further explanations of the questions or information required you should contact your named lottery officer. If more than 12 months have elapsed since you sent your *Advance Notice*, you should resubmit an updated *Advance Notice* before sending your application form.

ONCE YOU HAVE APPLIED

1. Acknowledgement of application

Once you have applied you should receive a letter acknowledging your application.

2. Consultation process

Your application will then be processed by your named lottery officer, who will consult with other relevant bodies (such as other Arts Council departments, your Regional Arts Board, the British Film Institute, the Crafts Council, or specialists in the field of access for people with disabilities). You may be contacted by your lottery officer if more information is needed about your plans.

If you have requested more than £100,000 of lottery funding from the Arts Council, it will usually appoint one or more independent lottery assessors to discuss your project with yourself or other relevant bodies, and in the light of this prepare a detailed report.

3. Decision by Arts Council of England National Lottery Board

Your lottery officer will then present the details of your application to the Lottery Board. The Board will make a recommendation to the Arts Council as to whether your proposal should be accepted or rejected. You will be informed of the final decision 'as soon as possible' – normally within six months of your application, or within four months for applications less than £100,000. Decisions on the first batch of grants will be announced by the end of March or start of April 1995.

CONTACT ADDRESS

Lottery Department
Arts Council of England
14 Great Peter Street
London SW1P 3NQ
Tel: 0171-312 0123
Fax: 0171-973 6571

SCOTLAND

The Scottish Arts Council has the remit for distributing the portion of the National Lottery proceeds to arts projects in Scotland. Decision-making power is primarily vested in the National Lottery Committee set up by the Scottish Arts Council. The committee's members are: Dr William Brown (chair), Fiona Walker (vice-chair), Dr Rita McAllister, Gordon Hallewell, Paul Dowds, Keith Geddes, Janette Richardson, Lesley Thomson, Dr Sheila Brock, Sheriff Peter Hamilton, John Denholm, Dr Ian McGowan, Robert Love, Professor Eric Spiller. The committee meets six times per year.

This committee makes decisions on applications requesting £10,000-£100,000, and also makes recommendations to the Scottish Arts Council which considers all proposals asking for £100,000 or more. The Director of the National Lottery, David Bonnar, has the power to make decisions in consultation with the Director of the Scottish Arts Council for applications asking for £10,000 or less.

ELIGIBLE BODIES

Organisations eligible for lottery funding from the Scottish Arts Council are: registered charities, non-profit distributing bodies, local authorities, colleges, universities, schools, amateur and voluntary arts groups. Commercial for-profit bodies may be eligible if their project is for the public good rather than for the organisation's commercial interests. Eligible bodies will usually be based in Scotland.

EXCLUDED BODIES

The main exclusions are: commercial organisations (for projects other than those primarily to benefit of the public); private individuals; organisations over which the Scottish Arts Council has material influence or control; and in the main, bodies based outside Scotland.

ELIGIBLE PROJECTS

Funding is available from the Scottish Arts Council's lottery funds for capital expenditure on arts projects and facilities located in Scotland, such as new building, building refurbishment, and the purchase of major items of equipment. Projects involving any area of the arts will be eligible, such as music, drama, dance, visual arts, crafts, film, literature, and any combination of the above (such as arts centres and festivals).

Funds may also be available for: feasibility studies or architectural design competitions involved with capital projects; individual film production projects; and the commissioning of 'Art in Public Places' (separate guidelines, criteria and application forms for these three areas are available from the Scottish Arts Council Lottery Department).

The Scottish Arts Council uses the following criteria when making decisions about applications for lottery funding:

Capital projects

Funding will normally only be available for capital projects on which work has yet to commence. Grants to support day-to-day running costs or create endowments to support such costs for a period not exceeding five years will only be considered if a project is of exceptional significance and has already received lottery funding towards its capital costs (in such cases you should contact the Lottery Director at an early stage of your application).

Minimum grant size: £5,000

The Scottish Arts Council is unlikely to consider applications for sums of less than £5,000.

Partnership funding

In general, no more than 75 per cent of the cost of any project will be provided by the Scottish Arts Council's Lottery Department, and for projects costing over £1 million it will provide no more than 50 per cent. The remainder of the finance should come from at least one other source, and cannot include any other distributor of lottery funds. The Scottish Arts Council states that 'while no fixed percentage of partnership funding will be required, all applicants will have to demonstrate that they have examined thoroughly other avenues of support'.

Public benefit

Your project should be of direct or indirect benefit to the public, and accessibility should be encouraged through adoption of a formal Equal Opportunities Policy and appropriate education and outreach activities. Full consideration should be given to facilitating the access of people with disabilities. If your organisation has a limited membership, such as a university or school, any lottery-funded project must be of significant public benefit or available for public use for a 'substantial period of time'.

Projects which fill the gaps

Priority will be given to projects which:

- Address the under provision of arts facilities outside the principal centres of population of Scotland.
- Improve or refurbish existing facilities within the principal population centres.
- Involve areas and art forms for which there is inadequate or underdeveloped provision within the principal population centres.
- Otherwise enable access to the arts to be developed beyond existing provision.
- Complement and enhance existing provision for the arts in relation to local, regional, or national arts development strategies.

The Scottish Arts Council requires that the demand for any planned facilities or services is illustrated by appropriate market research.

Financial viability

Your organisation must show that your proposed project is financially viable. In order to do so, the Scottish Arts Council requires that applications for between £100,000 and £500,000 of lottery funding provide a business plan and cashflow forecast, and those asking for more than £500,000 provide a fully worked up project and investment appraisal, cash flow forecast and business plan.

High quality of architecture and design

Priority will be given to proposals showing high standards of design and architecture, and which will make a significant and lasting impact on their surroundings and customers. Any building project should address the following criteria:

- Preparation of feasibility study
- Development of project brief
- Design quality
- Involvement of creative artists and craftspeople
- Energy efficiency
- Access for people with disabilities
- Project management
- Project costs
- Timescale
- Costs in use

Any application for £1 million or more of lottery funds will generally be expected to have conducted a competition to ensure the best possible standards of building design are achieved.

Effective management and marketing

Proposals should demonstrate an effective management structure, and a suitable promotion and marketing plan.

Other criteria

Applications for funding of feasibility studies or architectural design competitions, film production and art in public places are subject to further criteria which are specified in separate guidance notes available from the Scottish Arts Council.

EXCLUDED PROJECTS

Revenue funding

On the whole, only capital expenditure projects will be supported. Revenue and endowment funding will only be provided under exceptional circumstances.

Requests for grants of less than £5,000

The Scottish Arts Council will not normally use lottery funds to support requests for less than £5,000.

Projects outside Scotland

The Scottish Arts Council can only use lottery money to support projects which are located in Scotland. Arts projects in the other parts of the UK can apply to the other national Arts Councils for lottery funding.

Projects which have already commenced

Funding will only be provided for projects which have yet to commence.

APPLICATIONS PROCEDURE

1. Obtain application pack and relevant application form

The first stage in applying for funds is to obtain the application pack from the Scottish Arts Council Lottery Department at the address given below. This pack contains general information and separate application forms for building projects and equipment purchase. If you want to apply for funding for feasibility studies, architectural design competitions, film production or art in public places you will also have to request the relevant guidelines and application forms (which are *not* sent out with the normal application pack). You should then carefully check the eligibility criteria which are set out in the general information booklet.

2. Complete and return *Early Warning Form*
For applications for funding of £100,000 or more only

If you are going to apply for £100,000 or more of lottery funding from the Scottish Arts Council you should complete the *Early Warning Form* contained in the application pack, and submit it at the earliest possible opportunity. This form requests brief details about your organisation, the contact person, and the proposed project – in particular its estimated total cost, the amount you are applying for, and the likely date of returning the full application form.

Within one week of the Scottish Arts Council receiving your *Early Warning Form* you should be sent a letter of acknowledgement which will specify your Lottery Application Number. It will also identify the lottery officer who will be dealing with your application, and to whom all enquiries should be addressed.

3. Complete and return the appropriate application form

If you believe your organisation and project to be eligible for funding, the next stage is to complete and submit the application form suitable for the type of project you are proposing. [If you are requesting more than £100,000 of lottery funding from the Scottish Arts Council you should already have sent an *Early Warning Form* – Step 2 above].

There are five separate application forms available which cover:

- Building projects (including equipment and fixtures)
- Equipment purchase only
- Feasibility studies and architectural design competitions
- Art in public places
- Film production

It is most likely that your proposal will fall into one of the first two categories, and their application forms are summarised below. All questions on the application form should be answered, even if it is to state that the question is not applicable. Your answers should either be typed or handwritten in block capitals and black ink. Alternatively, you may use your own word-processing system (if you have one) and reproduce the questions in the same order with your corresponding answers.

Details of your organisation

Both the *Building Projects* and *Equipment Purchase* application forms begin with a section asking for details of your organisation, its management structure, and the contact person. You also need to state whether you are applying to another lottery distributor to help fund that particular project or purchase, whether you are seeking funding as part of a consortium, and whether you have/are already receiving lottery funding for any other project.

Project description/equipment details

Both forms then ask for information about the project/purchase you are proposing. The *Building Projects* form includes questions covering: the type of project; its location; the type of arts venue proposed and its anticipated pattern of use and audience; ownership of land/buildings; planning consents required; whether funding for any equipment, fixtures or fittings is required. The *Equipment Purchase* form has similar questions covering: the location and main function of the proposed venue for the equipment; details of the equipment required and its intended use; consultants appointed for advice; disposal of any existing equipment; building work which will be necessary to install the equipment and the planning consents required; the safety, lifespan and maintenance of the equipment.

Proposed benefits and demand for project/equipment

You are required to demonstrate how the project/equipment will increase the quality of artistic activity and otherwise benefit the area it serves . You need to give details about the catchment area, the estimated number of people who will use it, and the level of access the public will have to the project/facility. You have to show which relevant local authorities have been consulted, and the ways in which the project/equipment relate to arts development strategies.

Estimated costs and funding arrangements

The next section on the application forms deals with the estimated cost of the proposed project/equipment, the amount you are requesting from the Scottish Arts Council's lottery funds, and the planned or promised partnership funding.

Project management

You are required to specify preliminary work carried out, other preparatory work necessary, give a project timetable, and provide details of your plans for future management and revenue funding.

Architecture, construction and design (Buildings Projects only)

The *Buildings Projects* application form then requests information on project briefs and associated design competitions, and asks various questions about the quality of the proposed design.

Facilities for people with a disability

The final section on both forms asks you to demonstrate how you have taken the needs for disability access into account and whether you have consulted relevant groups. You have to complete a 23 point check-list about your commitment to providing access for people with a disability.

SUPPORTING DOCUMENTATION REQUIRED:

- A copy of your Constitution, Memorandum and Articles of Association, or any such document which describes your legally constituted status.
- A copy of your latest audited accounts and budget for the current financial year.
- A copy of any feasibility study, design brief or relevant market research report which has been completed.
- A copy of any Equal Opportunities Policy.
- A copy of your marketing plan *(building projects only)*.
- A detailed budget for the capital cost of the project.
- A detailed budget of operating/revenue costs covering a period of three full financial years after project completion/equipment purchase.

Applications for a sums of £100,000 or more should also provide:

- A detailed cashflow forecast covering the whole period of the project.
- A detailed business plan for your organisation covering the period starting from the next financial year and ending at least three full years after completion of the project.

Once you have completed the relevant application form you should send it, along with a copy of all supporting documentation, to the address shown at the end of this section. If you have any queries about the application form you should contact the Lottery Department on 0131-226 6051.

4. Deadlines

There are no deadline dates set for larger applications. These are accepted on a continuous basis and will be considered at the first Lottery Committee meeting following receipt of full application and after any necessary consultation has been undertaken. For applications involving requests of £10,000, however, your application will be dealt with most quickly (in 6-8 weeks) if you meet any of the following dates for submission: February 13th 1995; March 13th 1995; May 15th 1995; July 10th 1995; September 11th 1995; October 9th 1995; December 11th 1995; February 12th 1996.

ONCE YOU HAVE APPLIED

1. Acknowledgment of application

Within one week of the Lottery Department receiving your application form you should be sent a letter of acknowledgement. This will inform you of your application number and named Lottery Officer (if you had not previously sent an *Advance Notice Form*), and whether you had missed any essential information on your application.

2. Consultation process

The Lottery Department will then assess your application against its basic criteria. If it fails to meet any of the basic criteria it could be rejected at this stage. The Lottery Department may then consult with various bodies about your application, such as your local authority, the relevant Scottish Arts Council art form department, and disability organisations. An independent assessor may be appointed in certain cases, particularly for applications asking for more than £100,000.

Your Lottery Officer will keep you informed of the progress of your application and the likely timescale within which a decision may be reached. If you are asking for more than £100,000, he/she will also tell you the date of the Lottery Committee or Scottish Arts Council meeting which will consider your application.

3. Decision

Your application will then be considered by the Lottery Director, the Lottery Committee, or the Scottish Arts Council depending upon its size (see above). A decision should be made within 6-8 weeks for applications of £10,000 or below; within 3 months for applications of between £10,000 and £100,000, and within 4 months for applications in excess of £100,000 – although 'major projects' may take up to 6 months.

Once a decision is made, you will be informed in writing with one week, and unsuccessful applicants will be informed of the reason(s) for rejection.

If you wish to appeal any decision you should do so within two months of receiving notification of that decision. An appeal will only be considered if there was additional information not included in the initial application which might have materially influenced the decision. You may then be invited to submit this new information for the next decision-making session.

CONTACT

The Scottish Arts Council
Lottery Department
12 Manor Place
Edinburgh EH3 7DD.
Tel: 0131-226 6051
Help Desk: 0131-243 2444
Fax: 0131-220 2724

WALES

The Arts Council of Wales (Cyngor Celfyddydau Cymru) has been given the responsibility for distributing the Welsh share of the National Lottery proceeds for the arts. It has set up a Lottery Board consisting of Alwyn Roberts (chair), Jane Davidson, Hugh Hudson-Davies, and Geraint Stanley Jones. The Lottery Board considers applications for money and then makes recommendations to the Arts Council of Wales which makes the final decision. The Lottery Board is serviced by the Lottery Unit at the Arts Council of Wales, headed by Lottery Director Jo Weston, along with three Lottery Officers.

ELIGIBLE BODIES

Organisations eligible for lottery funding from the Arts Council of Wales are: registered charities, non-profit distributing bodies, local authorities, education institutions, public sector agencies. These organisations should be based in Wales and may be amateur or professional. In exceptional circumstances, a commercial for-profit organisation may be eligible to apply if its proposed project is primarily for the public benefit.

EXCLUDED BODIES

The main types of bodies which are not eligible for lottery funding from the Arts Council of Wales are: private individuals; commercial organisations (except in the cases outlined above); bodies not based in Wales; and any organisation under the effective control of the Arts Council of Wales.

ELIGIBLE PROJECTS

Lottery funding from the Arts Council of Wales is available for capital expenditure on arts projects and facilities located in Wales. This is taken to include: the purchase, improvement, restoration, construction or creation of buildings or equipment for the arts, as well as associated feasibility studies or architectural design competitions. Funding will be available for the widest possible range of arts forms and organisations, regardless of whether they have received other funding from the Arts Council of Wales in the past.

The Arts Council of Wales will take the following criteria into consideration when allocating lottery funds:

Minimum grant size: £2,000

Although it states that projects of all scales will be considered, the Lottery Board will 'not expect to give priority to applications for sums of less than £2,000'.

Public benefit and accessibility

Priority will be given to projects which can demonstrate the maximum likely benefit to the people and communities of Wales (across all regional, cultural, and economic sectors) resulting from their project. Accessibility should be enhanced through marketing, education and outreach activities, and full access should

ARTS

be given for people with disabilities. If your organisation has a limited membership (e.g. schools, universities), you will have to guarantee substantial community use.

Capital projects

Lottery funding from the Arts Council of Wales is only available for capital expenditure projects, such as the construction of new buildings, the enhancement of existing ones, and the purchase of equipment, vehicles and other capital assets. Limited amounts of revenue funding of day-to-day operation costs (for a period not exceeding three years) will be considered but only where a project is of exceptional significance or merit.

Project viability and management

Priority will be given to projects which have assured funding for running costs from other sources for a 'reasonable period' after completion (3-10 years), and which do not have an adverse effect upon your organisation's future financial stability.

Partnership funding

A maximum of 75 per cent of the total cost of any project will be available from the Arts Council of Wales' lottery funds and you will need to find the remainder from other sources (not including other Arts Council budgets or other lottery distributing bodies). For projects concerning groups or areas which can show a particular need, however, this maximum may be increased to 90 per cent of total project costs.

Quality of architecture and design

All planned building works should be of the highest possible standard of design with regard to accessibility, environmental impact, and energy efficiency. They should also complement the character of the local area and the nature of the facilities they house.

In order to ensure design quality, the Arts Council of Wales will normally expect all building projects requesting a grant in excess of £1 million to have undertaken a design competition. It will also consider applications for funding to support any design competitions necessary as part of a larger capital project.

Artistic quality and relevance to other plans

Applicants should demonstrate the quality of artistic activity likely to result from their project, the involvement of practitioners of the arts and crafts in their proposals, and the relevance of their plans to any local, regional, and national plans for arts development.

EXCLUDED PROJECTS

Projects located outside Wales

Lottery funding from the Arts Council of Wales is only available for projects and facilities located in Wales. Applications for projects based in England, Scotland or Northern Ireland should be submitted to the relevant national Arts Council.

Revenue funding

Apart from the exceptional circumstances outlined above, lottery funding from the Arts Council of Wales is only available for capital funding, and not to support revenue costs.

Applications for less than £2,000

The Arts Council of Wales gives a lower priority to application for less than £2,000.

APPLICATIONS PROCEDURE

1. Obtain *Guidelines for Applicants* pack

The first stage is to obtain the *Guidelines for Applicants* from the Lottery Unit at the Arts Council of Wales in order to check your eligibility. All documentation is available in both English and Welsh.

2. Obtain application form

If you consider your organisation to be eligible you should request the relevant application form either from the Lottery Unit or one of the Arts Council of Wales' regional offices (see Appendix VI). Separate forms are available for different types of projects, such as equipment purchase and construction of new facilities.

3. Complete and return application form

If eligible you will receive an application form carrying your Lottery Application Number. You should complete and return this form, which requests various details about your organisation, the proposed project, and funding for the project. You must either use this application form, or duplicate the questions and answers in exactly the same order on your own wordprocessor or typewriter (and you must remember to include your application number).

The information requested on the equipment purchase application form is fairly standard, and covers: details about your organisation; a description of the proposed project; the benefits of the project and the nature and size of the audience which will benefit; project costs and funding sources; and project management.

The completed application form and all supporting documentation should be sent to the address shown at the end of this section.

> **SUPPORTING DOCUMENTATION REQUIRED:**
> - A copy of your constitution or Memorandum and Articles of Association.
> - Your latest audited accounts and budget for the current financial year.
> - A copy of any feasibility study, design brief or relevant market research report which has been completed.

ARTS

AFTER YOU HAVE APPLIED

1. Acknowledgement of application

After the Lottery Unit has received your application you will be sent a letter of acknowledgement identifying the Lottery Officer who has been assigned to your application. You should contact your Lottery Officer if you have any enquiries about your application.

2. Consultation process

The Lottery Unit will then assess your application and consult with appropriate bodies such as art form and regional departments of the Arts Council of Wales, and other external specialist and umbrella bodies. Applications for grants greater than £100,000 will have an independent Project Assessor appointed to compile a detailed report on your plans.

3. Decision

The details of your application will then be presented by your Lottery Officer to the Lottery Board, which will make a recommendation for action to the Arts Council. You will be informed of the outcome as soon as possible. This should normally be within four months for applications involving less than £100,000, and within six months for requests for greater sums.

CONTACT

The Lottery Unit
Arts Council of Wales
Museum Place
Cardiff CF1 3NX
Tel: 01222-388288
Fax: 01222-395284

NORTHERN IRELAND

The Arts Council of Northern Ireland is the body with responsibility for distributing lottery proceeds to the arts in Northern Ireland. Its Board considers all applications and makes the final decisions regarding grant allocations, with administrative support provided by its Lottery Department.

ELIGIBLE BODIES

The following types of organisation are eligible for funding from the National Lottery Arts Fund for Northern Ireland: recognised charities; non-profit distributing bodies; local authorities; colleges, universities and schools; and other organisations, including commercial bodies, if their proposed projects are demonstrably for the public good. These organisations can be amateur or professional, and need not currently be funded by the Arts Council for Northern Ireland. Eligible bodies will usually be based in Northern Ireland.

EXCLUDED BODIES

The main exclusions are: private individuals; commercial organisations (if their projects are not primarily for the benefit of the public); any organisation over which the Arts Council of Northern Ireland has material influence or control; and, for the most part, organisations based outside Northern Ireland.

ELIGIBLE PROJECTS

The Arts Council of Northern Ireland uses its lottery funds to provide support for capital expenditure on arts facilities and projects located in Northern Ireland. This includes the construction of new buildings, renovation and refurbishment of existing facilities, and the purchase of major items of equipment. Projects involving any area of the arts will be considered, such as music, drama, dance, visual arts, crafts, literature, film, and arts centres and festivals.

It may also make funds available for feasibility studies and design competitions, film production and for public works of art. Separate application forms for these areas can be obtained from the Lottery Department.

The following criteria will be used by the Arts Council of Northern Ireland to assess applications for lottery funding:

Capital projects

As noted above, funds are usually only available for capital projects which have yet to commence.

Minimum grant size: £2,000

The Arts Council for Northern Ireland will not normally make any grants of less than £2,000.

Public benefit

All applicants should be able to show the benefit to the community that will result from their proposals. If your organisation has a restricted membership, or if you are a school, college or university, etc., you must make the project available for community use for a substantial period of time.

Demand for the project

Priority will be given to projects in any particular area which address a clear demand for facilities and resources which is not currently being met. This demand will need to be demonstrated by market research, and plans must be made to promote the facility or project effectively through education and outreach.

This means that the following types of projects will be given priority:

- New buildings or the development of new facilities in existing buildings which address underprovision.
- The improvement or refurbishment of existing facilities or buildings within principal cities.
- Projects involving areas of the arts where provision is currently inadequate or underdeveloped.
- The purchase of equipment which enables access to the arts to be developed beyond existing provision.

Partnership funding

The Arts Council will not use lottery funds to support the entire costs of any project. Instead it insists that partnership funding is obtained, as it will not normally provide more than 75 per cent of total project costs. In the case of feasibility studies and design competitions, only a maximum of 50 per cent of the cost will be available from lottery funds. Money from other Arts Council of Northern Ireland budgets or grants from other distributors of lottery funds cannot be counted as partnership funding.

Financial viability and effective management

The management of a lottery-funded facility or project must be effective and able to demonstrate public accountability. Applicants must also demonstrate that any project will be financially viable once completed, and that funds will be available to cover operating costs over an initial period. There are further requirements for larger applications: requests for between £100,000 and £500,000 of lottery funding must supply a business plan and cash flow forecast; and requests for more than £500,000 must supply a fully worked up project and investment appraisal, cash flow forecast and business plan.

Quality of design and architecture

Priority will be given to projects showing high standards of design and architecture, and which making a significant and lasting impact upon their surroundings and customers. Building design must also incorporate the fullest possible access for people with a disability, based on consultation with relevant groups. For requests of sums greater than

£100,000, the Lottery Department states that *firm preference* will be given to applicants who have based their proposals on a feasibility study. It will normally be considered *essential* for projects needing more than £1 million of lottery funds to undertake a feasibility study and a design competition or similar procedure.

Artistic quality and relevance to other plans

Projects should relate to local, regional and national strategies to develop the arts, and should improve the quality of artistic activity in the area.

EXCLUDED PROJECTS

Requests for grants of less than £2,000

Whilst stating that it will consider projects of all scales, the Arts Council of Northern Ireland will not normally give grants of less than £2,000.

Requests for grants of more than £2 million

The Arts Council of Northern Ireland also has a maximum grant size – it will not normally make any grants larger than £2 million.

Revenue funding

Revenue funding for day-to-day running costs will not normally be available. It will only provided under very exceptional circumstances and for a restricted period of time.

Projects outside Northern Ireland

The Arts Council of Northern Ireland will only distribute lottery funds to projects taking place in Northern Ireland. Requests for grants to support proposals in other UK countries should be addressed to the appropriate national Arts Council lottery department.

Projects which have already commenced

Funding is only available for projects which have yet to start, not those which are already underway.

APPLICATIONS PROCEDURE

1. Obtain *Application Guidance Notes* and application form

The first step is to obtain the *Application Guidance Notes* from the Lottery Department so you can check whether your organisation and project are eligible for funding. The standard information pack also includes application forms for building projects and equipment purchase – if you wish to apply for funding for feasibility studies, design competitions, film production, or commissioning public works of arts, you will have to separately request the relevant guidelines and application forms. When you are satisfied that your project is eligible you should move on to the next stage.

2. Complete and return *Early Warning Form*
For applications for funding of £100,000 or more only

If you are going to ask for £100,000 or more of lottery funding, you should complete and return the *Early Warning Form* contained in the standard information pack, and return it to the Lottery Department as soon as possible. This form asks for brief details of your organisation, the type of project you are proposing, its cost, other potential sources of funding, and the date you will be sending your full application.

On receiving your *Early Warning Form*, the Lottery Department will send you a letter of acknowledgement, which will state your Lottery Application Number to be quoted on all future correspondence (including your full application).

3. Complete and return the relevant application form

The next stage is to complete and submit the application form which is most appropriate for the type of project you are proposing. [N.B: If you are applying for more than £100,000 of lottery funding, you should already have submitted your *Early Warning Form*.]

Separate application forms are available for:

- Building projects (including equipment and fixtures)
- Equipment purchase
- Feasibility studies or design competitions
- Film production

As most applications are likely to fall into the first two categories, their application forms are briefly described below. You should answer all questions on the application form, even if it is only to state that the question is not applicable. The form may be typewritten or handwritten (in block capitals and black ink using extra paper where necessary). If you want you can also construct your own application form by reproducing all of the questions in the same order, with answers, on your own wordprocessing system (if any).

Details of your organisation

The forms start with a section which asks various questions about your organisation and the contact person.

Project/equipment details

The next section requests details of the building project or equipment purchase you are proposing, such as where it will be located and how it will be used.

Proposed benefits and demand for the project

You are then asked to show the ways in which the project will add to the artistic life of its neighbourhood. You need to show its potential audience size and catchment area, level of public accessibility, and plans for education or outreach work and marketing. You also have to give details of the proposed artistic programme.

Project costs and funding

The next section requests details of the total project or equipment cost, how much you require from lottery funds, and from where you expect to obtain partnership funding.

Project management

You then have to provide details concerning the management of your project both before and after completion, noting your timetable and main milestones, and showing how running costs will be met. Projects requesting more than £100,000 also have to provide a cash flow forecast covering the whole period of the project, and a detailed business plan for your organisation covering the period commencing with the next financial year and ending at least three full years after project completion.

Architecture, construction and design (Buildings only)

The application form for buildings projects then includes a section with questions about the process by which you have ensured the quality of the architecture, design and construction of your building project.

Facilities for people with a disability

Both application forms then conclude with a section covering your plans to provide access for people with a disability. The section includes a 23-point checklist covering various aspects of this topic which has to be completed.

Once you have indicated the supporting documentation you are providing, you should then sign the standard declaration. The completed application form along with supporting documentation should then be sent to the address shown at the end of this section. If you have any queries about the application form, you should phone the Lottery Department on 01232-667000.

SUPPORTING DOCUMENTATION REQUIRED:

- A copy of your Constitution or Memorandum and Articles of Association or any such document which describes your legally constituted status.
- A copy of your latest audited accounts and budget for the current financial year.
- A copy of any market research report that has been completed.
- A copy of any feasibility study or design brief that has been completed.

Additional documentation required for buildings projects:

- A copy of your marketing plan.
- A copy of any Equal Opportunities Policy.
- A detailed budget for the capital cost of the project.
- A detailed budget for operating costs covering at least three full financial years after project completion.

ONCE YOU HAVE APPLIED

1. Acknowledgement of application

When the Lottery Department receives your full application you will be sent a letter of acknowledgement, which will give your Lottery Application Number

ARTS

(although if you had already sent an *Early Warning Form* you should already know this and used it on your full application).

2. Consultation process

The Lottery Department will then assess your application against its criteria, and may consult with any body it considers appropriate (such as your Local Authority, the most relevant Arts Council art form department, or other specialist advisers and consultants). For larger applications, an independent assessor may be appointed to draw up a detailed report on your plans. You will be informed of the date of the meeting at which your application will be considered.

3. Decision

Once the consultation process is complete, the details of your application will be presented to the Board of the Arts Council of Northern Ireland. You will be notified of its decision as soon as possible.

CONTACT

Lottery Department
Arts Council of Northern Ireland
185 Stranmillis Road
Belfast BT9 5DU
Tel: 01232-667000
Fax: 01232-664766

CHARITIES

● ●

STRUCTURE

The National Lottery Charities Board was established from scratch in the National Lottery Act, as there was seen to be no pre-existing body with the capability for handling the size of money available from the lottery and the anticipated number of applications involved.

In the words of the Act, the Charities Board was set up to support 'charitable expenditure' both by charities and also

---

National Lottery Charities Board

Funding for charitable, benevolent and philanthropic groups throughout the UK in order to help 'meet the needs of those at greatest disadvantage in society and to improve the quality of life in the community.'

Likely minimum
size of application to
be considered: ... **£200** *for small grants programme*

Likely opening date for
first grant applications: .... **Mid 1995**

First grants likely to be announced: ...... **Late 1995**

---

institutions, other than charities, that are established for charitable, benevolent or philanthropic purposes. As such, eligible bodies include not just the 170,000 English and Welsh charities registered at the Charity Commission, and similar charities in Scotland and Northern Ireland, but also at least the same number of voluntary organisations. The Charities Board estimates that there may be as many as 700,000 extremely diverse groups eligible for assistance, which could lead to between 150,000 and 250,000 applications for funding per year – at least five times the estimated number likely to be received by the next largest distributing body.

The National Lottery Act specified that the Charities Board should consist of a chair plus 16 other members, with four committees serving in respect of England, Scotland, Wales and Northern Ireland. David Sieff was appointed as chair of the National Lottery Charities Board in May 1994. He is a director of high-street retailers Marks and Spencer (and great grandson of one of the firm's founders), and is a past-member of the Conservative Party's board of treasurers. The other Board members, announced in July 1994 by the Home Secretary, are listed in the box on the next page.

44

The National Lottery Charities Board has also appointed Timothy Hornsby as its chief executive, who previously performed a similar role for the Royal Borough of Kingston upon Thames.

Partially because there was no pre-existing structure upon which to build, but also because of the magnitude of the task involved, the Charities Board is lagging behind most of the other distributors by about 8-12 months. Its consultation process is getting underway at the start of 1995, doors opening for applications sometime after the Summer and the first grants not likely until the end of the year, although it is anticipating a phased start-up of its grant-making. Until the Board is ready to start giving out money, its share of the lottery proceeds will be held and invested by the National Lottery Distribution Fund – so there is no risk of the charities losing out because of the delays, despite press reports to the contrary.

As part of the consultation process, the National Lottery Charities Board has issued draft guidelines which give an idea of the type of organisations and projects it will and will not fund. This information forms the basis for the remainder of this section, but you should note that the guidelines are currently in *draft* from, so that there may be some variations between the criteria noted below and those actually implemented when the Charities Board issues its final policies after the consultation period.

The main aims of the consultation process are to gauge reactions to the draft guidelines and also to give an idea of the range, size and type of applications that the Charities Board can expect to receive. There are two aspects to the consultation process. The first is a survey conducted on a representative sample of over 7,500 charitable, voluntary and community organisations covering the whole of the UK. Each will be sent a questionnaire inviting them to give their reactions to the draft priorities and criteria produced by the Charities Board, and also their intentions to make any applications for funding. The results of this survey will be complemented by an open consultation exercise to be run at the same time. Any eligible organisation not included in the sample survey but which wants to make its opinions known can do so by requesting and completing a copy of the consultation questionnaire. The returned questionnaires from both parts of the consultation process will then be analysed separately. The results of both surveys will be used by the Charities Board when drawing up its final guidelines.

OVERALL AIMS

The main aims of the Charities Board are to help those who are socially disadvantaged and to enhance the general quality of life by enabling, supporting and encouraging charitable, benevolent and philanthropic organisations over the whole of the UK. By doing so, it hopes:

- To make the maximum possible impact on the lives of people suffering the effects of poverty, disadvantage and discrimination.
- To help prevent the emergence of new social problems; to tackle the causes of existing problems and address the needs they create; and to enhance opportunity and improve the quality of life.

- To devote part of its resources to supporting innovative and experimental initiatives.

In addition, it will aim to reflect the cultural and ethnical diversity found within the UK, and to be accessible to organisations and communities of all types and sizes, especially small and disadvantaged groups. The Charities Board does recognise, however, that some of the initiatives it will fund may fail, but considers this a price worth paying.

Part of the lottery proceeds will be split between England, Scotland, Wales and Northern Ireland on the basis of population figures weighted for disadvantage, although the precise manner by which disadvantage will be measured is not specified. Final decisions on applications from each of the home countries will be made by the appropriate Charities Board committee. The remainder of the lottery money will be used to support non-geographically specific projects and overseas development initiatives, and will be considered by the committee of the board covering the UK. The respective amounts which will be devoted to these areas have not yet been decided.

ELIGIBLE BODIES

Funding from the National Lottery Charities Board will be open to any organisation or group which has been set up for charitable, benevolent or philanthropic purposes. Applicants will usually have to meet a set of minimum qualification criteria, and should normally have a written constitution and a bank account with at least two signatories. You should also be willing to provide a set of your accounts. Exception may be made if your organisation is recently formed, although you will have to provide other evidence of commitment.

EXCLUDED BODIES

Public bodies (such as local and district councils) and private sector for-profit companies are not eligible to apply for funding, and individuals are not eligible to approach the Charities Board for money on their own behalf.

In addition, there are certain types of charitable activity which under the draft guidelines are not likely to receive support:

- Animal welfare.
- Medical treatment.
- Purely academic research.
- Primarily recreational activities.
- Primarily religious or missionary activities.
- Initiatives which are concerned exclusively with arts, sports or heritage activities (including revenue funding for such activities).
- Initiatives which would be eligible to apply for lottery funding from any of the distributing bodies for the arts, sports, heritage or Millennium projects.

ELIGIBLE PROJECTS

As noted above, the Charities Board has two main aims. Its priority is to concentrate upon initiatives which address the needs of, or provide opportunities to, individuals and groups who are at greatest disadvantage in society. In addition, it wishes to improve quality in life in communities, for example by improving both the physical environment and promoting citizenship.

Applications for funding will be evaluated against a set of priorities. The criteria and policies which are likely to be adopted by the Charities Board show some similarities to those used by the other distributing bodies, but there are several key distinctions. In particular, it *will* provide grants for revenue costs and not just capital expenditure, it does not require applicants to find other sources of partnership funding, and it is likely to make grants of only a few hundred pounds (see below). The main criteria which the Charities Board is likely to use in order to assess grant applications are listed below:

Both capital and revenue projects will be eligible

Unlike the other distributors of lottery money, the Charities Board will provide funding not only for capital support of buildings projects, equipment purchase and the like, but also for the *revenue costs* involved with running a project on a day-to-day basis.

Partnership funding not obligatory

Another major distinction compared with the other distributors is that you will not be required to find sources of partnership funding for your project. The Charities Board may, however, in certain instances give priority to projects which show potential for financial leverage of other monies.

Likely minimum grant size: £200

The Charities Board also expects to run a *small grants programme* alongside its programme for larger grants. This is likely to provide funding in the range of £200 to £2,000, which is much lower than the minimum limit applied by all other lottery distributors.

Benefit to the community

You must be able to show that your project will benefit the community and demonstrate the positive impact you expect it to have upon the intended beneficiaries.

Project viability

Your project should be well thought-out, financially sound and represent good value for money. It should also be sustainable in the long-term.

Other criteria

Where appropriate, the Charities Board may also employ some of the following criteria in assessing applications:

- Involvement of the community and users.
- Adoption of an appropriate equal opportunities policy.
- Originality of thought: the Charities Board will usually consider the degree to which your project shows strategic and innovative thinking, and whether it might be of value as a pilot project which could then be used by other organisations in similar circumstances.
- Inclusion of monitoring and evaluation procedures as an integral part of your project.
- The effective use of volunteers.

As noted above, the Charities Board will give priority to initiatives which address the needs of, or provide opportunities for, those who are of greatest disadvantage in society. Within this area, it expects to give preference to projects dealing with the following target groups:

- people suffering from the effects of poverty
- children and elderly people
- young people and young offenders
- people with a disability
- people suffering from mental or physical illness
- people who are unemployed
- ethnic and cultural minorities
- women's issues
- homeless people
- refugees
- people affected by alcohol or drug abuse
- people otherwise affected by discrimination

This list is not exclusive and may be increased to suit the needs of different regions.

Apart from initiatives concerned with combating disadvantage, the Charities Board will seek to improve the quality of life in communities. It will also aim to provide funding for projects and initiatives concerned with:

- overseas development
- developing and promoting the voluntary sector through activities such as training, dissemination of good practice, infrastructure support and community empowerment
- understanding and improving the local environment
- undertaking research and development work involving advances in technology which may be of benefit to disadvantaged people and groups.

In certain cases, the Charities Board may also consider providing assistance in making applications for support. In the longer-term it also hopes that it will be able to make available, as a general resource to the voluntary sector, the benefits of its grant-making experience and professional knowledge in the fields it supports.

EXCLUDED PROJECTS

No replacement of statutory funding

You should not request money from the Charities Board in order to replace statutory funding.

Requests for less than £200

The Charities Board is unlikely to consider any applications below its minimum limit of £200.

APPLICATION PROCESS

At the time of writing, information was not available concerning the Charities Board's application process, even in draft form. The main details will become clear as the consultation process continues.

It looks likely, however, that there will be some degree of devolution of decision-making powers, given the four committees established for England, Scotland, Wales and Northern Ireland. The Charities Board states that it aims to 'devolve decision-making to the level closest to the beneficiaries'.

Precise criteria and procedures are likely to vary between countries and even between regions. The Board's draft guidelines note that: 'Different countries and regions will clearly encounter a diverse geographical spread of deprivation, whether it be focused on rural areas, the inner city, areas of industrial decay, peripheral housing estates or whatever.' It is thus likely that different criteria will be adopted according to the nature of deprivation found in a region. The proportion of money to be set aside for the small grants programme in each country will also be determined autonomously within that country.

CONTACT ADDRESS

If you want any information about the consultation process or the draft guidelines, you should contact the Charities Board at the address given below:

National Lottery Charities Board
7th Floor, St Vincent House
30 Orange Street
London WC2H 7HH
Tel: 0171-839 5371
Fax: 0171-839 5369

CHARITIES

HERITAGE

· ·

STRUCTURE

The share of the National Lottery proceeds earmarked for the benefit of the heritage is distributed by the *Heritage Lottery Fund*. The Heritage Lottery Fund is controlled by the trustees of the National Heritage Memorial Fund, a separate fund which was established in 1980 to provide financial assistance for the national heritage as a memorial to those who have given their lives for the country – this fund now operates in tandem with the Heritage Lottery Fund.

> ## The Heritage Lottery Fund
>
> *Funding for 'capital projects which safeguard and enhance public access to land, buildings, items and collections considered to be of interest to the local, regional and national heritage of the United Kingdom.'*
>
> Minimum project size
> normally considered: **£10,000**
>
> Opening date for
> grant applications: .... **January 4th 1995**
>
> First grants
> announced: .... **April/May 1995**

The chair of the National Heritage Memorial Fund (NHMF) is Lord Rothschild, and its trustees are Sir Richard Carew Pole, Lord Crathorne, Lindsay Evans, Sir Nicholas Goodison, Caryl Hubbard, Sir Martin Jacomb, John Keegan, Lord Macfarlane, Professor Palmer Newbould, Mrs John Nutting, Catherine Porteous, and Commander Michael Saunders Watson. From January 1995 they are responsible for distributing the Heritage Lottery Fund alongside the Heritage Memorial Fund. The Heritage Lottery Fund is administered from offices in London by a team headed by Rosemary Ewles.

Unlike the lottery funds distributed by the national Sports and Arts Councils, which are split in advance between the four countries in the UK according to population size, the Heritage Lottery Fund will not be allocated in any predetermined way across the home countries. The NHMF states that: 'Although we will not attempt to allocate funds based on relative populations in advance we will carefully monitor our expenditure to ensure balanced coverage of the UK is being achieved over time. If it appears that insufficient applications are coming forward from particular counties or regions we will assess the reasons for this and consider whether special steps need to be taken to advise and encourage potential applicants.'

The NHMF is also likely to hold a series of regional briefings in Spring 1996 in order to get feedback on the activities of the Heritage Lottery Fund after its first full year of operation.

HERITAGE

ELIGIBLE BODIES

Organisations eligible for support from the Heritage Lottery Fund are those which are public, charitable or non-profit distributing, based in the UK and have the preservation or conservation of the heritage in this country as one of their purposes.

These eligible bodies will thus include:

- 'Any museum, art gallery, library or other similar institution having as its purpose or one of its purposes the preservation for the public benefit of a collection of historic, artistic or scientific interest.
- Any body having as its purpose or one of its purposes the provision, improvement or preservation of amenities (including ancient monuments and historic buildings) enjoyed or to be enjoyed by the public or the acquisition of land to be used by the public.
- Any body having nature conservation as its purposes or one of its purposes.
- The Secretary of State for National Heritage.
- The Department of the Environment for Northern Ireland acting in discharge of its functions relating to the acquisition of historic monuments or listed buildings by agreement.'

EXCLUDED BODIES

The excluded bodies are private individuals, organisations established or conducted for profit, and any institution established outside the UK.

ELIGIBLE PROJECTS

The primary aims of the Heritage Lottery Fund are to secure, conserve, improve, and enhance public access to and appreciation of *'tangible heritage assets'*. These are buildings, land, objects or collections which are of importance to the heritage whether in a local, regional or national context. The term 'asset' is used by the NHMF to reflect the nature of these items: they are tangible resources which add to the overall 'wealth' of the national heritage.

The NHMF defines five main types of heritage asset, each with their own detailed guidelines (see below), although it recognises that there is often considerable overlap:

- Ancient monuments, historic buildings and their contents and settings
- Land of scenic, scientific or historic importance, including the designed landscape
- Special library collections, manuscripts, archives and other records

- Collections held by museums and galleries
- Buildings, sites and objects associated with industrial, transport and maritime history.

The Heritage Lottery Fund will thus be used to finance projects concerned with any of these types of heritage asset. Projects should result in 'tangible benefits to tangible assets', and there are the following eligibility criteria:

Local, regional or national heritage importance of project

The project should concern heritage assets of importance on a national, regional or local scale.

Consolidation rather than innovation

The Heritage Lottery Fund will be primarily used in order to enhance and consolidate existing heritage assets and heritage provision, rather than for the creation of new institutions or the reconstruction of past heritage.

Public benefit and access

All applicants must be able to show the public benefit that would result from their proposed project. Projects should enhance public access to and enjoyment of heritage assets.

Capital projects

In keeping with the Secretary of State's policy directions, the Heritage Lottery Fund will be directed almost exclusively at capital projects. These are projects which involve direct capital expenditure on purchase, improvement, restoration, construction or creation of a tangible asset, including any costs directly connected with these activities.

The Heritage Lottery Fund does have powers to make endowment or revenue funding available for lottery-funded projects, but expects to use this ability 'very sparingly'. Money will only be distributed in revenue grants or for the purposes of endowments where these costs are associated with capital projects already funded by the lottery and whose completion would be prevented by the lack of any other suitable source of revenue or endowment finance.

Project viability

Applicants need to be able to show that sources of funding have been identified which will provide support after lottery funding has ceased. As revenue costs and grants for future maintenance are not available from the Heritage Lottery Fund, applicants should be able to demonstrate how these will be met from other sources. Applicants should also have sound finances and a reasonably secure future.

Partnership funding

The Heritage Lottery Fund will not provide 100 per cent of the costs of any project. It expects applicants to provide a significant element of partnership funding, or contributions in-kind, from non-lottery sources. The NHMF states that it will be 'flexible' in determining what constitutes a significant element as it realises this will vary according to the situation of the applicant and the nature of the project. It does state, however, that there should always be some contribution from the applicant's own resources, and that the Heritage Lottery Fund will normally expect to make up 50-75 per cent of total project costs.

Minimum project cost £10,000

The NHMF states that the Heritage Lottery Fund will consider both 'large and small' projects. In general, however, the Heritage Lottery Fund will only consider applications for projects with a total cost of £10,000 or more (although this figure is being kept under revue). Projects with a total cost below £10,000 may, however, be eligible where the applicant can show both genuine need (in particular that there are no appropriate sources of public funds) and that the project of importance to the heritage.

Other criteria

Applicants must show their need for lottery support and in particular that their project would be unlikely to succeed without the support of the Heritage Lottery Fund. The project, or phase of work, should not yet have commenced, and the work proposed should be realistically costed and of good quality with regard to design, construction, historical integrity, and professional and technical standards.

New buildings or projects should provide the fullest possible access for people with disabilities, although the NHMF recognises that there may be constraints to full access in certain kinds of projects (such as listed buildings).

If the proposed project would normally be eligible for priority funding from other public funding sources, it is likely to be given a lower priority by the Heritage Lottery Fund unless the project would fail without lottery support.

Applicants are also responsible for obtaining the necessary planning or other statutory consents necessary to enable the project to be carried out. No grant offer will be made by the Heritage Lottery Fund without evidence of all such consents being secured.

Examples of eligible projects

The NHMF gives the following examples of the types of projects which are eligible for support from the Heritage Lottery Fund:

- Acquisition, repair, conservation or restoration of buildings, land or objects of importance to the heritage.
- New buildings, or improvements to existing buildings, designed to house museum or archive collections of importance to the heritage, or to improve public access to any kind of heritage asset.

- Listing or cataloguing of archives or collections of objects, or the recording of sites and buildings, where these can be demonstrated to be finite projects resulting in a significant enhancement of public access to and better preservation of the assets concerned.
- Any other capital project which aims to improve public access to, and understanding and enjoyment of, such buildings, land, objects and collections.

There are also specific criteria which apply to each of the five categories of heritage asset defined by the NHMF:

1. Ancient monuments, historic buildings (and their fittings, furnishing and contents) and historic sites.

Eligible projects in this category include the acquisition, major repair, conservation, or restoration of: town and country houses, places of worship, civic buildings, domestic, agricultural and garden buildings, funerary monuments, memorials and statues, and sites, buildings and structures important to the heritage of archaeology, industry, transport, maritime or defence. The installation of appropriate visitor facilities to promote the public appreciation of such sites and buildings are also included.

These sites and buildings, and their settings, should be of recognised importance to the national heritage, which may be indicated by scheduled, listed, graded or registered status, or location in a Conservation Area.

2. Land of scenic, scientific or historic importance

Eligible projects in this category include the purchase, restoration, preservation, enhancement, interpretation of, or the enhancement of public access to, land of geological, biological, historic or scenic importance to the national heritage, which includes parks, gardens, and land including archaeological sites, monuments or historic buildings. This land should be of recognised importance to the heritage, either by virtue of officially designated status or otherwise identified as locally or regionally important.

3. Printed books, manuscripts, archives and other records, and the buildings in which such collections are housed

Eligible projects include the acquisition of items or collections of artistic, historic or scientific interest and importance to the national heritage, such as manuscripts and archives, special library collections, photograph, sound and film archives and other records. Applicants must be able to show that any items or collections purchased will be appropriately conserved and made available for public study or display.

The construction, extension, conversion or major refurbishment of buildings and facilities for housing such collections are also eligible, as are the installation of appropriate security, fire and environmental monitoring and control systems in such buildings. Projects involving new buildings, repositories or collections will normally only be considered if the NHMF is advised that they would fill a major gap in present provision, either on a geographical basis or in a specific subject area.

The listing, cataloguing and conservation of collections will normally only be eligible if these activities can be shown to be 'capital' projects, i.e. they could only be achieved with the assistance of lottery funds and that they are beyond the normal scope of the applicant's budget.

4. Museum and gallery collections

Eligible projects include the purchase, conservation, cataloguing, housing and display of collections of importance to the national heritage held in galleries and museums. These include collections of: fine and applied art, archaeology and antiquities, ethnography, local and social history, military history, industry, science and technology, biological and geological collections, and collections of historic buildings in open-air museums. The Heritage Lottery Fund will be utilised to encourage good practice by supporting museums with access to professional staff and which meet the minimum standards of operation defined by the Museums and Galleries Commission.

Conditions are fairly similar to those outlined in the previous category – projects involving the construction of new buildings, extensions and conversions in order to house such collections are eligible in order to provide suitable conditions, as are cataloguing and conservation if they are 'capital' projects. Additionally, applicants should be able to show that the proposed project is outside the scope of the capital funding provided by the Museums and Galleries Commission and the ten Area Museums Councils covering the UK, and that lottery funding is vital to the projects' success.

5. Industrial, transport and maritime heritage

Eligible projects include the acquisition, repair, conservation, restoration and housing of very large objects of industrial, scientific and technological importance to the national heritage, such as ships, vehicles, aircraft, railway items, and other machinery. Buildings and sites of such importance are covered by Category 1 above. The condition and completeness of any object will usually be one of the factors taken into consideration.

Projects involving the return of objects to working order will only be considered where the NHMF is assured by their experts that the proposals will not damage the historical integrity of the item and that subsequent maintenance by the applicant is guaranteed. The Heritage Lottery Fund will also cover the costs of any dismantling, transport or reassembly involved in the acquisition of a particular object. The applicant should also be able to guarantee that any statutory safety standards will be met.

Any proposals should take into account the appropriate best practice outlined by the Museums and Galleries Commission, as the Heritage Lottery Fund will be used to promote similar activities.

EXCLUDED PROJECTS

Revenue funding

The Heritage Lottery Fund will not normally assist projects other than those which are only concerned with capital expenditure (see above). As a result, projects requiring assistance for revenue funding (such as training or general research programmes) will not normally receive help.

Projects with a cost below £10,000

Projects with a cost below £10,000 are not eligible to apply unless both genuine need and importance to the heritage can be demonstrated.

Excavations

The Heritage Lottery Fund will not normally fund archaeological, paleontological or geological excavations and recording projects unless these are a necessary consequence of a lottery-funded capital project.

Regeneration projects

Projects involving the creation of a new landscape, or the creation of heritage assets where none currently exist will not normally be considered – this rules out, for example, projects involving the regeneration of urban derelict lands.

The NHMF gives the following examples of projects which are **not** eligible for assistance from the Heritage Lottery Fund:

- Training programmes
- Temporary exhibitions
- Marketing initiatives
- Educational, interpretive or conservation facilities not associated with specific heritage assets
- General research projects, unless closely related to a particular heritage asset
- Libraries – the Heritage Lottery Fund will not support local authority lending library services. (It will, however, consider projects involving special library collections of rare books or unique collections, as specified above.)
- Publications, in any medium, not associated with a lottery-funded listing or cataloguing project

- Archaeological excavations
- Regeneration of derelict urban land.

APPLICATIONS PROCEDURE

1. Read the *Heritage Lottery Fund: Simple Guide*

The first step in order to apply for funds from the Heritage Lottery Fund is to request the *Heritage Lottery Fund: Simple Guide* and complete its eligibility check which consists of the questions listed in the box below.

2. Request the *Guidelines and Applications Pack*

If you are able to answer 'yes' to all of the below questions, you should be eligible for support from the Heritage Lottery Fund, and so the next stage is to request the *Guidelines and Applications Pack* from the National Heritage

ELIGIBILITY CHECK FOR HERITAGE LOTTERY FUND

We are a public sector organisation, a charity or a voluntary organisation concerned with the preservation and presentation of buildings or land or objects or collections of importance to the UK heritage, and we are based in the UK .... ☐ YES ☐ NO

Our application concerns an existing 'heritage asset' or 'assets' based in the UK .... ☐ YES ☐ NO

The project (or phase of work) for which we are seeking support is in the future and has not already commenced .... ☐ YES ☐ NO

It is a clearly defined capital project of the following type:

acquisition .... ☐ YES ☐ NO

or repair, conservation or restoration .... ☐ YES ☐ NO

or new building or improvement to existing building .... ☐ YES ☐ NO

or improving access to, and understanding and enjoyment of buildings, land, objects or collections .... ☐ YES ☐ NO

We will secure partnership funding from other sources .... ☐ YES ☐ NO

The total cost of the project is over £10,000 .... ☐ YES ☐ NO

Following investigation we believe that our project is unlikely to succeed without the support of lottery funds .... ☐ YES ☐ NO

Our project will enhance the public access to and enjoyment of our 'heritage asset' or 'assets' .... ☐ YES ☐ NO

HERITAGE

Memorial Fund (address given below). If you are not sure about the eligibility of your project it is also worth consulting this pack as Guidelines are explained in fuller detail. There is a request form for the Guidelines and Applications Pack on the back of the Simple Guide, which also asks you to complete a few simple questions about your organisation and, if possible, the project for which you are likely to make an application.

3. Check the Guidelines

Having received the Guidelines and Application pack you must read the Guidelines carefully to check the eligibility of your project. If you have any queries about eligibility you should contact the Heritage Lottery Fund on 0171-930 0963.

4. Complete the application form

Before filling in the application form you must check that there is an application number in the box on the top right hand corner of its first page. If there is no number the application form is not valid and it will not be accepted by the NHMF. The application form is fairly short, but requires extensive supporting documentation.

Details about your organisation

The form kicks off with a few simple questions about the application, and then asks for information on your organisation, such as your official name, address, the date your body was established, and your charity, company or VAT number (where appropriate). It also requests information about the contact name and address for all correspondence concerning the application.

Project details

The form then requests information on the name and location of the project for which funding is necessary, along with a brief 150 word description of the project. This section requires substantial supporting documentation, specified below.

Project timetable and planning permissions

You also need to provide details of when the project is expected to start and finish, and information about planning permissions or statutory consents applied for, granted or expected.

If you have a particularly urgent deadline to meet, for example for the purchase of an item which will be going on sale on a specified date, the Heritage Lottery Fund has a 'fast track' for urgent cases. In this situation you should notify them as soon as possible, if necessary by telephone initially, and follow this up as soon as possible with your application form.

Project costs and funding sources

The next section asks for details of the total estimated project cost, along with the estimated value of any non-cash contributions (such as land, materials or

HERITAGE

MAIN SUPPORTING DOCUMENTATION REQUIRED

- Copy of audited accounts for the last two complete financial years.

- First-time applicants should supply a copy of Rules, Trust Deed, or Memorandum and Articles of Association as appropriate.

- First-time applicants should also include a brief description of the organisation, its management structure, and the number of trustees or board members.

- The collecting policy of any institution applying for funding for acquiring a collection or archive.

- Evidence that the named contact is authorised to act on behalf of the applying body, such as a copy of committee minutes.

- Detailed project description, including an assessment of its importance to the national heritage (such as whether it is officially designated, for example as a listed building), and whether the application is in any way urgent as the asset concerned is under threat. This should be accompanied by plans, illustrations, maps, diagrams, and photographs as appropriate. At this stage do not send any video material or three-dimensional items (such as models) but indicate if these are available.

- A description of the short, medium and long-term benefits which should accrue from the project when it is completed.

- A description of how public accessibility will be maximised, including access for people with disabilities. Where possible this should include an estimate of the additional number of individuals, and types of user, who will benefit from the project.

- Copies of any feasibility study, design brief, technical or conservation report, restoration or management plan relevant to the project.

- Details of any local, regional or national strategies which would support the project.

- Details of the key professionals/companies who will be involved in the project, such as architects, surveyors, conservators, ecologists.

- Where and when the project or item can be inspected by the National Heritage Memorial Fund or its advisers.

- A detailed timetable for the project, if available, which should include information about phases of work.

- A clear indication if the project for which you are applying is just one phase of a larger programme of work.

- Details of any projects your organisation will be running at the same time.

- Details of how project running costs will be met once lottery funding has ceased.

voluntary labour) included in this total figure. You have to specify the amount you wish to receive from the Heritage Lottery Fund – bearing in mind that it will not fund the whole of any project costs – and provide evidence of partnership funding from your own resources and from other sources. For acquisition projects, the form asks for two independent valuations of the item. You are also required to state whether your organisation has applied to the Heritage Lottery Fund or any other lottery distributor now or at any time for any part of this project or any other project, and to provide details if you have.

There are two types of project for which additional information is required, apart from that specified above:

Projects with total cost over £500,000

Apart from projects involving the straightforward acquisition of objects, all projects with a total cost of £500,000 or more are required to submit a business plan along with their application. The standard application pack supplied by the NHMF includes the 10-page booklet: *Heritage Lottery Fund: Guide to Preparing a Business Plan*. This provides a useful starting-point if your organisation needs to draw up a business plan for its lottery application.

Projects involving new buildings, extensions, conversions and refurbishments

Heritage construction projects should provide a design report which considers the following points, where appropriate:

- Why the new building is necessary.
- Sources of advice used when producing the design brief and how the architect or designer was or will be chosen.
- If new buildings to house collections or archives are involved, there should be an indication of sources of conservation advice used and the impact of the building design on the environment for collections.
- Methods of procurement employed.
- How the project will be managed, and how much it will cost to run.
- Forms of public consultation used.
- Quality of construction and materials used.
- A consideration of access to the building for people with disabilities.

5. Send your application to the Heritage Lottery Fund

The following items should be submitted to the Heritage Lottery Fund at the address given at the end of this section:

- Two copies* of the completed application form (one can be a photocopy).
- Two copies* of the supporting documentation, all of which should be marked clearly with the name of the applicant organisation and project name.
- Two copies* of a covering sheet which should list all supporting documents enclosed with the application – these should identify which document refers to which question on the application form.

[* The second copy will be passed to one of the Heritage Lottery Fund's advisers.]

If at any stage of the application process you have any queries, you should contact the Heritage Lottery Fund Department on any of the following numbers: 0171-747 2087/6/5/4/3/2

ONCE YOU HAVE APPLIED

1. Confirmation of your application

You should receive confirmation of your application within 14 days of it arriving at the NHMF offices. This acknowledgement will:

- Confirm that your application is eligible.
- Inform you of the unique reference number given to your application.
- Indicate the date of the trustees' meeting at which the application is likely to be considered.
- Give you the name of the Lottery Case Officer assigned to your application. This is the person you should ask for if you have any enquiries about the decision-making process, quoting your application reference number.

2. Consultation process

The Heritage Lottery Fund will then seek expert advice on your application on which the trustees of the National Heritage Memorial Fund can base their decision. This advice will normally come in the first instance from the relevant public advisory body. In the case of applications concerning historic buildings, for example, these may include English Heritage, Heritage Scotland, Cadw: Historic Buildings and Monuments in Wales, or Department of the Environment, Northern Ireland. Advice may also be obtained from other specialist bodies and independent experts where appropriate. This process may involve a visit by a Heritage Lottery Fund adviser to discuss and/or visit the project involved.

3. The decision

If your application is eligible, a decision on whether it will receive assistance should be made by the NHMF trustees within 5 months of its receipt. You will then be notified of the trustees' decision within 7 working days of the meeting at which your application was considered.

This decision will fall into one of the following categories:

- *Approved for support*
  For projects which are fully approved a formal offer of a grant will be made and sent to you along with a copy of the associated terms and conditions.

- *Conditionally approved*
  Approval may only be granted conditionally, for example subject to you raising other elements of partnership funding, or if there is a requirement for the submission of detailed plans, or if there are adjustments to proposals. In such cases you will normally have 12 months in which to meet your specified conditions, after which you will have to submit a new application.

- *Not approved for support*
  Some applications will inevitably be considered unsuitable for funding and be rejected. If you are unsuccessful and want returned any photographs, plans, drawings or other supporting documentation submitted with your application, you should contact the NHMF within 6 months. In other cases your application may not be approved for support because the trustees are temporarily unable to make further future commitments of lottery funds. If this is the case they will advise you to try again within a certain period.

If you are unhappy with this decision you should write in the first instance to Georgina Nayler, Director of the National Heritage Memorial Fund. If you are still not satisfied, you have the right to ask an MP to take up your case on your behalf, which could even lead to the case being referred to the Ombudsman if there is evidence of possible maladministration (if this happens it will not cost you anything for the Ombudsman to look at your case).

CONTACT ADDRESS

Heritage Lottery Fund
National Heritage Memorial Fund
10 St James's Street
London SW1A 1EF.

Application enquiries: 0171-747 2087/6/5/4/3/2

NHMF general telephone number: 0171-930 0963

HERITAGE

MILLENNIUM

The Millennium Commission

Funding for projects which assist communities in marking the year 2000 and the beginning of the third millennium, taking any of the following forms:

- *Large capital projects of national or regional significance.*
- *Smaller capital projects of local significance.*
- *Millennium Festival.*
- *Millennium Bursary Scheme.*

Minimum size of project normally considered:
Landmark capital projects: .... £10 million
Local capital projects: £100,000
Festival and Bursary details not yet available

Opening date for applications:
All capital projects: .... January 4th to April 30th 1995
Festival and Bursaries: .... Late 1995

First grants announced:
All capital projects: .... July/August 1995
Festival and Bursaries: .... not yet known

STRUCTURE

The Millennium Commission was created by the Secretary of State in the National Lottery Act to receive one-fifth of the good cause proceeds. Its aim is to fund projects which 'mark the year 2000 and the beginning of the third millennium'. It will receive money from the lottery until December 31st 2000, after which date the proceeds will be split four ways between arts, sports, heritage and charities.

Like the National Lottery Charities Board, the Millennium Commission has been set up from scratch, as there was thought to be no suitable pre-existing organisation which could act as a distributing body. The membership of the Millennium Commission was set down in the Act as consisting of nine individuals, two of who are Ministers of the Crown and one nominated by the Leader of the Opposition. These 'commissioners' are appointed by the Queen on the recommendation of the Prime Minister, and are listed in the box on the following page.

The Millennium Commission has, however, encountered a few problems since inception. The first difficulty was to pin down exactly what was meant by the former Heritage Secretary, Peter Brooke, when he said in June 1994 that funding will go to projects that are *'of the millennium'*. His successor, Stephen Dorrell, has commented, 'It's a bit like an elephant, you recognise it when you see it', although some of his fellow commissioners seem less sure. When Heather Couper was told that the general public was confused, she reportedly replied: 'So are we'.

The other problem was the very public dismissal of the Commission's high profile chief executive-designate Nicholas Hinton, who had previously been director general of Save the Children Fund. He was released from his contract just days before he was meant to have started his new job in October 1994, apparently because he proved incompatible with nine very 'hands-on' commissioners. The vacancy will now be filled by Jennifer Page, who takes over as chief executive of the Millennium Commission at the beginning of March 1995 having formerly fulfilled a similar role at English Heritage since 1989.

MILLENNIUM COMMISSION MEMBERS

Stephen Dorrell MP   Chair of the Millennium Commission; Secretary of State for National Heritage since July 1994.

Michael Heseltine MP   President of the Board of Trade.

**Professor
Heather Couper**   Astronomer, writer and broadcaster.

Earl of Dalkeith   Son and heir to one of the UK's wealthiest landowners, the Duke of Buccleuch, and director of the Buccleuch Estates and its Heritage Trust; also regional chair of Scottish Natural Heritage and member of the Independent Television Commission.

Robin Dixon CBE   Heir to Lord Glentoran and managing director of Redland (Northern Ireland) Ltd and chair of Positively Belfast. Past Olympic gold medal winner in the bobsleigh.

Sir John Hall   North East property developer and chair of Newcastle United FC.

Simon Jenkins   Journalist and former editor of the *Times*.

Michael Montague CBE   Nominated by the Leader of the Opposition. Businessman and past chair of both the English Tourist Board and National Consumer Council.

Patricia Scotland QC   Barrister, first black woman QC, and former member of the Race Relations Committee of the General Council of the Bar.

MILLENNIUM

After a process of consultation, the Millennium Commission has stated its intention to support four main types of project:

Large capital projects of national or regional significance

The Millennium Commission intends to fund around one dozen very large capital projects of national or regional importance spread across the UK, each to the tune of between £10 million to £50 million. These projects are expected to become landmarks for the 21st century, and will account for the largest share (about 50 per cent) of the Millennium Commission's funding.

Smaller capital projects of local significance

The Commission will also fund a larger number of smaller capital projects of local significance with contributions in the range £100,000 to £15 million. Applications will also be considered from consortia with joint proposals for schemes with a common theme that might otherwise be too small for consideration.

Millennium Festival

The Commission will finance a Millennium Festival or Exhibition which it wants to be a focus for celebrations in the year 2000. Whilst no further details are currently available, the Commission is consulting as to what form this festival might take, and will publish its conclusions in Spring 1995.

Millennium Bursary Scheme

The Commission is currently developing a Millennium Bursary Scheme to provide funding for the fulfilment of 'more personal aspirations' for the next century. The exact form of this bursary scheme is not yet apparent, as no further details are currently available and applications cannot yet be made.

ELIGIBLE BODIES

The following types of organisation are eligible to apply to the Millennium Commission for capital projects to mark the year 2000:

- Registered charities.
- Non-profit distributing bodies.
- Local authorities and other public bodies, where the application does not substitute for public expenditure.
- Commercial or for-profit organisations, but only if projects are for the public good rather than private gain.
- Consortia or partnerships of eligible bodies specifically established for the purpose of submitting an application.

EXCLUDED BODIES

The main exclusions are that individuals are not eligible to apply for funds on their own behalf, and neither are private sector organisations if their proposals are for commercial gain rather than for the public good.

ELIGIBLE PROJECTS

When the Millennium Commission is considering applications for projects to mark the millennium it will take the following criteria into account:

As indicated above, the Millennium Commission is at present only inviting applications for capital projects to mark the year 2000 which are locally, regionally or nationally significant. The rest of this chapter is concerned only with applications for projects of this type, and not the Millennium Festival or Bursary Scheme.

Marking the millennium

Projects should look back over the current millennium or forward into the new one, and have the potential to be viewed by future generations as marking a significant moment in local or national history. This is possibly the most difficult of the criteria to fulfil, as it is still not very clear exactly what the Millennium Commission has in mind to celebrate the year 2000.

Completion date

The Commission normally expects that any proposals considered in the 1995 tranche of applications should be operational in the year 2000.

Primarily capital projects

The Millennium Commission funding is primarily available for capital funding toward projects designed to mark the new millennium. This includes expenditure on the purchase, restoration, construction or creation of an asset, as well as expenditure on improvements designed to extend an asset's lifespan, capacity, quality or value.

Funding thresholds

The Commission states that it normally expects to keep its contribution toward total project costs within the following ranges: £10 million-£50 million for the dozen landmark capital projects of national or regional significance, and £100,000-£15 million for projects of local significance. Thus, unless you are part of a consortium, your project must require at least £100,000 from the Millennium Commission to be considered.

Partnership funding

The Millennium Commission will not provide funding for the total costs of any project, as it requires an element of partnership funding from other non-lottery sources. The Commission will not normally provide more than 50 per cent of the cost of any proposal, although in exceptional circumstances this contribution may be increased. A high proportion of both revenue and capital funding from other sources will be interpreted as an indication of greater community support for your project.

Public good

One essential requirement is that projects should be for the public good and accessible to the general community for a substantial part of the time. They must make a substantial contribution to the life of the community they are designed to serve.

Long term viability and effective management

Your project must be a viable concern once Millennium Commission funding has finished, and you should be able to meet running costs for a reasonable period following completion from other sources. You should be able to provide a cash flow forecast, fully worked-up project and investment appraisals, and a business plan. The project should also be effectively managed both before and after completion.

Quality of project

Your proposals should demonstrate a high standard of design, architecture and environmental quality. Buildings should be environmentally sound, energy efficient, and fully accessible to people with a disability.

MILLENNIUM

Other primary sources of funding unavailable

Applications will normally only be considered if they are not eligible for funding from any of the other distributors of lottery funding or statutory sources. Projects should not be possible without the support of the Millennium Commission.

If you wish to apply for funding from the Bursary Scheme or your proposal is for a Millennium Festival, the following advice and guidelines do not apply. You should contact the Millennium Commission to ascertain whether the appropriate information is yet available.

EXCLUDED PROJECTS

Revenue funding

As Millennium Commission funding is primarily available for capital expenditure, projects are excluded if they are mainly asking for revenue funding.

Projects requiring less than £100,000 of Millennium Commission funding

The Millennium Commission expects its usual contribution to be greater than £100,000, even for projects of solely local significance. Unless your organisation is part of a larger consortium, if you request an amount smaller than £100,000 your application is likely to be rejected.

Projects requiring more than £50 million of Millennium Commission funding

The Commission will not normally make any contribution greater than £50 million towards any project, even if it is of national significance.

APPLICATIONS PROCEDURE

Unlike most of the other distributing bodies, the Millennium Commission is administering the applications it receives on the basis of annual competitions for grants, with deadlines for submission at the end of April each year. Applications received after this date will be returned to you, although you can re-submit them for consideration in the next year's grants round. The procedure for applying for funding for a capital project of local, regional or national significance is outlined below.

1. Obtain *Introduction to the Millennium Commission*

The first step is to obtain a copy of the *Introduction to the Millennium Commission* leaflet from the Commission on 0171-340 2001.

2. Obtain *Proposal Form and Guidance Notes*

The *Introduction to the Millennium Commission* leaflet contains some basic information about the Commission and its funding strategy, but more importantly also includes a tear-off slip which you should fill in and return in order to receive a Proposal Form Pack, consisting of *Guidance Notes* and a *Proposal Form*.

3. Submit *Proposal Form*
Before March 31st 1995 for 1995 grants competition
Autumn 1995 – March 31st 1996 for 1996 grants competition

If, having read the *Guidance Notes*, you consider that you have a project suitable for funding by the Millennium Commission, the next stage is to submit a *Proposal Form*. N.B. You must submit this proposal form by the end of March in the year you wish your full application to be considered. The *Proposal Form* asks you to summarise the main features of your proposed project, including its funding sources. You do not have to state whether your project is for a national/regional project or a more local one, as the Commission will make this assessment when considering your full application later. The completed *Proposal Form* should be sent to the address shown at the end of this section.

You can send a covering letter with this form, but it should be no longer than 2 pages. If you send any other detailed information it will be returned to you.

4. Receive acknowledgement of *Proposal Form*

The Millennium Commission will send you a letter to acknowledge receipt of your *Proposal Form* and will give you a Unique Project Reference number which should be quoted in all future correspondence. You should receive this letter within 10 days of sending your proposal to the Commission.

5. Receive results of initial consideration

After sending you a letter of acknowledgement, the Commission will then consider your proposal form. You should receive a letter within three weeks of submitting your proposal, informing you of the outcome which will take one of two forms:

- If your proposed project meets Millennium Commission requirements you will be sent an application pack and details of the project team dealing with your full application. You are then free to apply for funding.
- If your proposal is not seen to meet their requirements, you will receive a letter informing you of that decision. The Commission does *not* think that you would be wise to spend more time and effort in completing a full application. You are not prohibited from doing so, however, and you can still request an application pack if you so wish.

6. Submit *Application Form* and details of your project
Before April 30th 1995 for 1995 grants competition
Sept 1995 – April 30th 1996 for 1996 grants competition

The final stage is to complete and return your *Application Form* along with details of your project. You must submit your *Application Form* by the end of April in the year you wish it to be considered in the grants competition. If you send it after that date it will be returned to you, although you can re-submit it for the next year's competition.

The Millennium Commission's application form for capital projects is one of the shortest of any of the distributing bodies, and asks for brief details about your organisation and your project. This is because you also have to submit a *short document* setting out the main features of your project – this should be no longer

MILLENNIUM

than 20 pages of A4 accompanied by any maps, diagrams or drawings which are required to illustrate the text.

The main aspects which you should cover in this document are:

Project Overview

You should give a full description of the proposed project including details about: how the project was conceived and what it involves; the benefit it will provide to the community and the estimated number of users or visitors; its national, regional or local significance; and the degree of public support.

Project implementation

You should show how the project will be implemented, the organisations involved, and the development timetable. You also need to demonstrate how design and environmental issues have been taken into account, and whether European procurement regulations apply.

Project finance

You must give details of the total project cost, and how funding will be provided, including the size of contribution required from the Millennium Commission. An outline project plan should also be given along with a detailed financial appraisal.

Land and assets required

Give information about any land or assets that you might need to purchase, any planning permissions required or gained, and any infrastructure issues which will need to be addressed.

Post implementation stages

You should also give details about the future use and management of the project, including predicted running costs and how these will be met.

> **Supporting documentation required:**
> - A copy of your audited accounts for the last two years and your two most recent annual reports, if available.
> - Evidence that the named contact person is authorised to act on your organisation's behalf.
> - A copy of your Trust Deed, Memorandum and Articles of Association, or other appropriate governing material.
> - Names and addresses of all sources of partnership funding.
> - Names and addresses of all sources of revenue funding.
> - Contact names and addresses for planning and other matters in your local authority.

The application form includes a checklist of points you should include in your project description. You may not be able to provide all of the information requested if you have not yet conducted a full feasibility study or you have experienced delays in the planning proces. If this is the case, you should give details of how you expect to proceed. If any details are missing, your application will still be considered but no grant will be made until the Commission is satisfied on all points.

Your application form and project document should be sent to the address shown at the end of this section.

ONCE YOU HAVE APPLIED

1. Receive acknowledgment of application

Once the Millennium Commission has received your full application, you should receive a letter of acknowledgement.

2. Application assessment process

Your application will then go through a four part assessment process:

- First, it will be checked against the Commission's criteria for projects (summarised above).
- Second, the Commission will seek independent advice on the financial viability and technical feasibility of your application. It will also confirm the sources of partnership funding, and seek the views of your local authority with regard to the planning and other implications of your proposals.
- Once these first two hurdles have been successfully cleared, other public or advisory bodies may then be consulted for their views on individual aspects of your project.
- Finally, all of the applications received for that year's grants competition will be considered together. The Commission will then decide which of them merit further assessment, and which should be rejected at this stage.

You will be informed of the Commission's decision at this stage (which will probably be reached by the end of May). You should, however, be aware that just because the Millennium Commission believes your project to be worthy of further consideration it will not necessarily receive funding.

3. Site visits

If your proposal has been identified for further consideration, the Commission will arrange a visit to your site, and set up a meeting between your representatives and the Millennium Commissioners or their staff. These will probably take place in June and July.

4. Shortlist stage

Once the site visits and meetings have taken place, the Millennium Commission will look at all the applications which it thought worthy of further consideration. It will then make a decision as to whether your application should be:

• *Accepted, in principle, as a Millennium Project*

You will then be placed on a shortlist for an offer of a grant to be made, pending availability of lottery funds. You will be informed of the expected date upon which money will be available, at which point a formal offer of a grant will be made. If you have been shortlisted, you should receive the first grant payment in September.

• *Asked to undertake further preparation*

You may be asked to undertake a feasibility study, raise further partnership funds, provide an investment appraisal or business plan, or undertake other further preparation before a final decision is made. The Commission will identify whatever extra work is required, and set a deadline for its completion. It may consider contributing a proportion of the costs of this work (but this does not necessarily mean that your application will definitely be accepted).

• *Rejected*

Even if your application has reached this stage of the assessment process, it is still quite likely to be rejected.

If at any stage of the application or assessment process you have any questions you should contact the Millennium Commission on 0171-340 2001. The Commission will also hold a series of workshops in February and March 1995 for applicants who have passed through the *Proposal Form* stage. Everyone who receives an Application Pack from the Commission will be informed of workshops in their area, at which they should be able to iron out any difficulties with applications under preparation.

CONTACT ADDRESS

Millennium Commission
2 Little Smith Street
London SW1P 3DH
Tel: 0171-340 2001

Deadlines and key dates for 1995:

31 March Deadline for receipt of Proposal Forms for consideration in 1995 grants competition. Proposals received after this date will be returned to their sender, although may be re-submitted for the 1996 grants competition after September 1995.

30 April Deadline for receipt of Application Forms for consideration in 1995 grants competition. Applications received after this date will be returned to their sender although may be re-submitted for the 1996 grants competition after September 1995.

End of May Identification of applications for further consideration.
Rejection of unsuitable applications.

June & July Site visits and meetings for projects identified for further consideration.

End of July Decisions announced:
Shortlisting of projects waiting for offers of grants.
Identification of applications requiring more work before a final decision is made.
Rejection of unsuccessful applications.

September First instalments of 1995 competition grants paid. Start of 1996 competition.

SPORTS

STRUCTURE

The share of the lottery proceeds which is to benefit sport is being distributed by the Sports Councils of England, Scotland, Wales and Northern Ireland. The allocation of money between the countries was determined in the National Lottery Act 1993 according to relative population levels, as follows:

- Sports Council (England)   83.3%
- Scottish Sports Council   8.9%
- Sports Council for Wales   5.0%
- Sports Council for
  Northern Ireland   2.8%

The Lottery Sports Fund in England will thus receive the bulk of the money generated by the National Lottery for sports in the UK.

The Sports Councils for England, Scotland, Wales and Northern Ireland

Funding for capital projects which increase active participation in sport and recreation

Minimum total project size normally considered:
£5,000 (England)
£10,000 (Scotland)
£5,000 (Wales)
£5,000 (Northern Ireland)

Opening date for applications:
January 4th 1995 (England)
January 4th 1995 (Scotland)
January 30th 1995 (Wales)
January 4th 1995 (Northern Ireland)

First grants announced:
Spring 1995 (England)
Spring 1995 (Scotland)
April/May 1995 (Wales)
Spring 1995 (Northern Ireland)

ENGLAND

The portion of lottery proceeds which is to benefit sport in England is being distributed by the Sports Council. Final decisions on applications are made by the Sports Council National Lottery Grants Panel, who are all Sports Council members, and administrative back-up is supplied by the Sports Council Lottery Unit.

ELIGIBLE BODIES

Lottery funding is only available to sports which are *recognised* by the Sports Council – if your organisation's activities are not included in the list shown below you will not be able to apply. And for those which are starred (*) you must be affiliated to your sport's national governing body for safety reasons.

ACTIVITIES RECOGNISED BY THE SPORTS COUNCILS

Aikido*
American football
Angling
Archery*
Arm wrestling
Association football
Athletics
Australian rules football
Badminton
Ballooning*
Baseball
Basketball
Baton twirling
Bicycle polo
Billiards and snooker
Bobsleigh*
Boccia
Bowls
Boxing*
Camogie
Camping and caravanning
(under review)
Canoeing*
Caving*
Chinese martial arts*
Cricket
Croquet

Crossbow*
Curling
Cycling
Disability sports
Dragon boat racing
Equestrian*
Fencing*
Fives
Flying*
Gaelic football
Gliding*
Golf

Gymnastics*
Handball
Hang/para gliding*
Highland games
Hockey
Horse racing
Hovering
Hurling
Ice hockey
Ice skating
Jet skiing*
Ju jitsu*
Judo*
Kabaddi
Karate*
Kendo*
Korfball
Lacrosse
Lawn Tennis
Life saving*

Luge*
Modern pentathlon*
Motor cycling*
Motor sports*
Mountaineering*
Movement, dance, exercise
and fitness*
Netball
Orienteering
Parachuting*
Petanque
Polo*
Pony trekking
Pool
Quoits
Racketball
Rackets
Racquetball

Rambling
Real tennis
Roller hockey
Roller skating
Rounders
Rowing
Rugby league
Rugby union
Sailing/yachting*
Sand and land yachting
Shinty
Shooting*
Skateboarding
Skiing*
Skipping
Snowboarding*
Softball
Sombo wresting*
Squash
Street hockey

Sub-aqua*
Surf life saving*
Surfing*
Swimming
Table tennis

Taekwondo*
Tang soo do*
Tenpin bowling
Trampolining*
Triathlon
Tug of war
Unihoc
Volleyball
Water skiing*
Weightlifting*
Wrestling*
Yoga

SPORTS

With this provision in mind, the following types of organisation are eligible to apply for funding from the Lottery Sports Fund, as long as they are based in and operate in England:

- Voluntary sports clubs – if membership is open to all and the constitution clearly states that a recognised sport is a primary purpose of the organisation.
- Area sports associations – if composed of local sports clubs involved in recognised activities.
- National governing bodies – but only those which are recognised by the Sports Council.
- Local authorities and other public bodies.
- Charitable trusts, playing fields associations, youth clubs, and community associations – but only if a recognised sport is part of the constitution and public access will be provided to the facility.
- Schools, colleges, and universities can only apply if their proposals are not just for curricular activities, and if the proposals will help resolve a real shortage of facilities. There must be guaranteed public access of more than 40 hours a week backed up by a Community Use Agreement.
- Commercial organisations and professional sports clubs are only eligible if their proposals will provide a benefit to the community which cannot be met otherwise. Any such facility cannot be run for profit, must be available to the public for at least 40 hours each week and be subject to a formal Community Use Agreement.

EXCLUDED BODIES

Sports not recognised by the Sports Council are not eligible for funding, and individuals cannot apply for money for their own benefit. And, in general, commercial bodies and professional sports clubs are excluded unless their projects are for the public benefit and not their commercial gain. In addition, children's play activities will not be considered initially, although 'mini' versions of recognised sports are eligible. Organisations not based in England or not providing benefit in England will normally be excluded – those based in the other home countries should apply to their relevant Sports Council.

ELIGIBLE PROJECTS

Lottery funding from the Sports Council will be 'almost exclusively' for capital projects aimed at increasing active participation in sport and recreation, either directly or through the provision of support facilities.

Examples of such projects are:

- Construction of new buildings and facilities.
- Genuine upgrading, expansion or modernisation of existing facilities.
- Purchase of land, water, sporting rights or other facilities for immediate use (but not land or facilities for *future* use or development).
- Provision of changing rooms for participants and officials (with equal opportunities in mind).
- Provision of support facilities such as safety equipment, storage facilities, conditioning rooms, childcare facilities, landscaping and boundary fences, and car parks, access roads, and access for people with disabilities.

Lottery funding will not normally be available for equipment purchase, but in certain cases, this will be eligible if the equipment is a necessary part of a larger capital project eligible for lottery funding; or it is major item which will be used for at least five years and permanently based on-site; or it will comprise a pool of equipment for a single sport or for more than a local area.

The following criteria are applied by the Sports Council when assessing applications for lottery money:

Capital funding

As detailed above, money is only available for capital projects. Lottery money will not normally be available to support on-going revenue costs associated with salaries, maintenance, heating, cleaning, etc. In exceptional cases, however, an application for revenue funding may be considered if connected with a capital project already supported by the Lottery Sports Fund, and needed for specific start-up costs which cannot be met from other sources. The project will have to be judged a high priority by the Sports Council, and even so will only provide revenue funding for no more than three years.

Minimum total project size: £5,000

The Sports Council will not normally consider applications involving projects with a total cost of less than £5,000. Small projects may be considered, however, if they will be of long-term importance to the sporting community and if alternative sources of funding are not available.

Backers of projects with a total cost of more than £5 million should discuss their application as soon as possible with the Sports Council.

Partnership funding

The Sports Lottery Fund will only provide a maximum of 65 per cent of the total costs of any project, and would prefer at least half the costs to come from other sources. It expects your organisation to supply some of this funding, normally a minimum of 10 per cent if you are a voluntary organisation. Your contribution does not have to be in cash, and it could take the form of donated land and materials, or the equivalent value of volunteer work. The Sports Council states that if you manage to increase the proportion of money from non-lottery sources above the minimum level this is 'bound to help your application'.

Financial viability

Your project should be financially viable in terms of funding from all sources, and properly managed both during the course of the project and in the longer-term. You are expected by the Sports Council to provide a business plan of your future projections, which in most cases can be quite basic although you might be asked to provide a more detailed appraisal.

Project quality

Your proposals should be of high quality and able to withstand many years of use, and should meet the appropriate sporting standards imposed by the Sports Council and other national sports governing bodies. They should meet statutory requirements and any appropriate specifications for lighting, ventilation and heating. Any facility must provide full access for people with disabilities, and otherwise be designed and built to a high standard.

Preparations in place

Your project should be ready to start as soon as possible after a Lottery grant has been awarded. You should not be too hasty, however, as the Sports Council will not consider your proposal if any contracts for building works have already been signed.

Breadth of appeal and support

Your project should address the needs of the widest possible cross-section of the community – the more people who stand to benefit from your proposal, the greater its chance of lottery funding. Preference will also be given to projects which will increase the participation of people who are at present denied access to sport and recreation. In certain cases you will also be required to demonstrate how the need for community access can be appropriately balanced with use by elite performers for training.

You should also obtain support for your proposals from as many different communities and organisations as possible, and in particular local, regional, and national sports bodies.

Relevance to other plans and facilities

Wherever possible, your application should be in line with sports strategies drawn up by local authorities, regional and national sports governing bodies (including the Sports Council). The Sports Council does recognise, however, that applications may arise which challenge existing priorities or come from sports or areas where there are no existing strategies. Your proposals should also take full account of the relationship with similar facilities which already exist in your area or sport.

EXCLUDED PROJECTS

Revenue funding

The Sports Council will not normally provide lottery finance for day-to-day running costs, except in the circumstances outlined above.

Equipment

Lottery funding will not normally be available for the purchase of small-scale items of equipment, including mini-buses and equipment for personal use.

Maintenance

The Sports Council will not provide lottery funds for maintenance, repairs, renewals, or any other work which is necessary as a result of past neglect. In certain cases it might, however, provide funding for major items of maintenance equipment.

Spectator facilities

As the Lottery Sports Fund has the aim of increasing active participation in sport, backing will not initially be given for projects solely concerned with spectator or social accommodation. These facilities may be funded, however, if they comprise a necessary part of a larger scheme, such as the development of strategically important venues.

Projects with a total cost of less than £5,000

As noted above, the Lottery Sports Fund will normally consider only those applications involving projects with a total cost of £5,000 or more.

Projects based outside England

Projects which are not based in England will not normally be funded.

APPLICATIONS PROCEDURE

1. Obtain application pack

If you think your organisation may wish to apply for lottery funds for a sports capital project, the first step is to obtain an application pack from the Sports Council by phoning their Lottery Line on 0345-649649 (charged at local rate for whole of the country). You will receive an application pack along with your unique reference number.

2. Send *Consultation Forms* to relevant bodies

If, having read the *Guidelines for Applicants*, you consider your organisation and project to be eligible for funding, you can then start the application process proper. If you need further information on sports building, planning, design and management, the Sports Council produces a series of general publications and guidance notes for individual sports. You should send the *Consultation Forms* contained in the application pack to all organisations relevant to your project: the national governing sports bodies (form A), other national organisations (form A), local authorities (form B), county playing fields association (form C), local sports council (form C). These consultation forms ask the organisations to state whether they are, or will be, giving your organisation any financial support, how your project fits into any strategic plans, and what priority they would place on the scheme.

These forms should be sent to the appropriate bodies a few weeks before you submit your application to the Sports Council. They will fill them in and direct them straight to the Sports Council (and not return them to you).

3. Complete and return application form

The next stage is to complete the application form provided by the Sports Council. All sections should be completed, and answers should either be typed or handwritten in black ink and preferably in block capitals. The application form is also available on computer disk, if you prefer to submit your proposal in that way. The main sections of the application form are as follows:

Applicant's details and previous lottery funding

You are first asked to give details about your organisation and its status, and the main contact for correspondence about your application. You are then asked if your organisation has undertaken any previous applications (successful or otherwise) for lottery funding.

Project and site details

The next section requests information about your proposed project, including a brief description, its nature, the sport(s) which will significantly benefit, start and finish dates, and the existence of any existing facilities on the same site. You also have to give details of site location, ownership, and any planning permissions necessary or granted.

Usage of facility

You are then asked to give details of the number of regular active users of existing facilities, and the approximate increase in sports participation if your proposals go ahead. There are also questions about the current users of your facilities, as well as your current coaching facilities, catchment area, and charges. You have to give information about the level of public accessibility to your proposed facilities and how access will be granted.

Project cost and funding

The following section asks for the anticipated total capital cost of your project, and how this estimate is calculated. You also have to show other sources of capital funding for the proposals, and also how any future revenue costs will be met.

Technical details

This section requests the names of any professional advisers you have consulted when drawing up your proposals, such as architects, engineers, surveyors, solicitors and accountants. There are also questions covering accessibility to the project on the grounds of gender and disability. The form concludes by asking you to set out what you hope to achieve through the project, how you intend to do this, and how you will measure progress.

Supporting documentation required

- A copy of the Constitution or Memorandum and Articles of Association for your organisation.

- A copy of your latest annual accounts and balance sheet.
- Project brief.
- Proposed site plan (where applicable).
- Schedule of proposed equipment (where applicable).
- Draft lease (where applicable).
- Letters of confirmation for project finance.
- Detailed income and expenditure projections.
- Any evidence relating to the breakdown of your project costs.

Additional documentation for building projects only:
- Feasibility study (where applicable).
- Building drawings and/or A4 size sketch drawings (whichever are available).

Once the application form has been completed it should be sent along with one copy of any supporting documentation to the address shown at the end of this section. If at any stage of the application process you have any queries you should telephone the Lottery Unit on 0171-388 1277 (Monday-Friday, 2pm-5pm only).

ONCE YOU HAVE APPLIED

1. Acknowledgement of application

Once the Sports Council has received your application form it will send you a letter of acknowledgement.

2. Consultation process

Your application will be evaluated by one of the Lottery Unit's lottery case officers according to the criteria laid out in the Sports Council's documentation (summarised above). There will be a process of consultation with relevant national, regional and local bodies, and the relevant Sports Council regional office will offer its comments.

3. Decision by Sports Council National Lottery Grants Panel

Once the period of consultation has been completed, your application will go before the Sports Council National Lottery Grants Panel with a recommendation. The panel will then make its decision, and you will be informed of this outcome 'as soon as possible'. There are three possible outcomes:

- Grant award – you will receive a formal offer of a grant, along with the relevant conditions.
- Provisional grant award – a provisional offer of a grant will be made, pending a more detailed appraisal (normally for larger or more complex proposals only).
- Rejection – if your application is not successful you will receive a letter with the reasons for rejection (where appropriate). You can ask for a review of this decision if you have suitable grounds. Otherwise you cannot re-apply within 12 months of the rejection of an earlier application.

CONTACT ADDRESS

Lottery Unit, Sports Council
PO Box 649, London WC1H 0QP
Lottery Line: 0345-649649 for application packs
Tel: 0171-388 1277 for advice on applications 2pm-5pm
Fax: 0171-387 1999

SCOTLAND

The Scottish Sports Council is responsible for distributing proceeds of the National Lottery to promote sports in Scotland. It has set up the Lottery Sports Fund Unit to deal with the administration of applications, headed by the director of lottery operations, Ivor Davies. Final decisions on grants are made by a meeting of the Scottish Sports Council.

ELIGIBLE BODIES

The Scottish Sports Council will only provide lottery funding to bodies involved with sports which are already *recognised* by the Sports Councils (SEE TABLE 73). Your organisation should be Scottish based and involved with increasing sports participation in Scotland. In addition, your organisation can be any of the following:

- Local voluntary sports clubs – as long as your constitution states that a recognised sport is a primary purpose. User groups representing consortia of local recognised clubs are also eligible.
- Area sports associations – but only those with a constitution and composed of local clubs of recognised sports.
- National governing bodies of sports – but only those recognised by the Scottish Sports Council as the sole body for that activity in Scotland.
- Charitable trusts, playing fields associations, youth and uniformed associations, and community associations – but only if the playing of sport is an object in your constitution, your membership is open to all parts of the community, and significant public access will be provided to the project or facility.
- Local authorities and other public bodies.
- Quasi-commercial organisations which re-invest all surpluses back into the project or facility (rather than distributing profits to managers or shareholders).
- Universities, colleges, schools and other educational establishments – but only if the proposed facility will be available to local sports clubs and the general public for a significant amount of time. This should normally be at least 50 per cent of opening hours or available playing time.
- Professional sports clubs and commercial organisations are only eligible if their projects will bring about significant benefits to the community whilst not providing commercial benefit to the organisation. In the case of commercial bodies, there should be no other organisation capable of providing the facility.

EXCLUDED BODIES

As noted above, professional sports clubs and commercial organisations are excluded from seeking funds for any project involving significant commercial gain. Bodies which are not based in Scotland, or which do not benefit the country, are also excluded. Individuals are not eligible to apply for funding on their own behalf.

ELIGIBLE PROJECTS

The Scottish Sports Council is focusing its lottery funds on capital projects which are for the public good and will provide a lasting benefit to the community. The Council also aims to spread its support over the entire range of sports, at all scales, and in all parts of Scotland.

Preference is being given to projects which promote participation in sport and improve sporting performance, and fill the 'high priority deficiencies' identified by the Scottish Sports Council in terms of existing knowledge and strategies. The Council cites the following specific types of facility being given priority:

- sports halls
- upgraded turf pitches
- indoor tennis courts
- upgraded outdoor tennis courts
- synthetic grass pitches
- changing pavilions
- swimming pool upgrading
- pay-as-you-play golf courses
- various resource-based developments.

As well as trying to rectify these current deficiencies in Scottish sports provision, the Council will adopt a further priority ranking based on the type of project. This ranking is shown in the box opposite, in order of stated preference.

In general, the following additional criteria will be used by the Scottish Sports Council when it is assessing applications:

Capital funding

As noted above, the Scottish Sports Council will normally fund only those sports projects involving 'expenditure on the purchase, improvement, restoration, construction or creation of an asset', including any costs (such as professional advisers' fees) directly incurred in the process. In certain cases, money may be available for feasibility studies or design competitions necessary prior to the submission of a full application for a major capital project.

Revenue funding for day-to-day running costs will not normally be provided, although it may be provided in exceptional circumstances for specified time periods and purposes to support projects which have been granted support for large-scale capital expenditure.

Minimum total project cost: £10,000

The Scottish Sports Council is initially concentrating its lottery funds on applications involving projects with a total project cost of £10,000 or more. It also has a maximum grant level of £1 million which it will only exceed in very exceptional circumstances.

SPORTS

HIGHEST PRIORITY

- Development (construction, extension or improvement) of playing facilities, including those for natural resource-based activities.
- Acquisition or retention of playing facilities, such as purchase of land or rights of access.
- Plant (water treatment, heating, lighting, ventilation, booking systems) for sports facilities.
- Major sports equipment – usually large and/or expensive, but with a long life span (of at least seven years).
- Changing accommodation for participants.
- Facilities and equipment for sports medicine and science.
- Equipment storage in new developments.
- Facilities for sports officials – which should be essential for performance and not just comfort.
- Conditioning suites for participants, where they are an essential feature of sports facilities and consistent with applicable sports plans or strategies.
- Crèches to enable greater sports participation.
- Dual social and activity areas, dependent upon a clear benefit to sports.
- Access facilities such as car parking which are in balance with, and essential to, sports facilities.
- Boundary fences necessary for safety and security.
- Spectator accommodation – but only at facilities of national and regional importance and where consistent with sports development strategies.
- Landscaping – where it is as an essential part of new facilities.
- Residential or overnight accommodation at key locations.

LOWEST PRIORITY

Partnership funding

The Council will normally only provide a maximum of 75 per cent of the total capital costs of any project, with the remainder coming from your own organisation or other non-lottery sources of money. Initially, however, the level of capital award from the Council will not exceed 50 per cent of eligible costs depending on need, up to a maximum grant level of £1 million.

Financial viability during project and after completion

You should be able to demonstrate that your project is financially viable, both during and after its completion.

Increase in sports participation and relationship with other strategies

Proposals should increase participation in sports and recreation, or provide improvements in performance. There should be a clear demand for the planned facilities, which should relate to other community programmes and initiatives.

Fit for purpose

Any proposed facilities must be 'fit for purpose' in terms of their location, scale, content, design and construction, accessibility for people with disabilities, management, and environmental impact.

EXCLUDED PROJECTS

The main types of projects which are not eligible for lottery funding from the Scottish Sports Council are:

Revenue projects

In general, revenue funding will not be provided (although under exceptional circumstances it may be available, see above).

Repairs

Lottery funding will not be used to pay for repairs, renewals or maintenance brought about by prior neglect.

Small scale items of equipment

Only the purchase of major items of equipment will normally be funded – minor items, including items of equipment for personal use, mini buses, vans and other vehicles, will not receive support from lottery proceeds.

Social facilities

Dedicated social areas, dining rooms or bars not connected to participants' residential accommodation will not normally be funded . Neither will free-standing administration areas or committee rooms which do not comprise an essential part of large sports projects.

Spectators' facilities

Because lottery funds are being used to promote active participation in sport, funding will not be available for spectators' facilities unless part of a major capital project.

Projects outside Scotland

Projects located outside Scotland are not eligible, and should approach their relevant national Sports Council.

Projects with a total cost below £10,000

Small-scale projects with a total cost of less than £10,000 will initially be unlikely to receive lottery money.

SPORTS

APPLICATIONS PROCEDURE

1. Obtain application pack

The first stage is to request the guidelines and application pack from the Scottish Sports Council. If you expect your project to have a total cost of £1 million or more, you should contact the Lottery Sports Fund Unit to inform them about your project before applying.

2. Complete and return application form

Applications should be made on the official form supported by all relevant documentation. If the answers are not typewritten, the form should be completed in black ink using block capitals. The main sections of the form are as follows:

Details of your organisation and any previous lottery funding

The first section on the form asks for details about your organisation, such as its status (e.g. registered charity, voluntary body, company, local authority, etc.) and affiliation with any of the national governing bodies of sport. You must also state whether your organisation has previously applied for, or received, any lottery funding. If your organisation is a club with individual members you also have to provide information about the composition of your membership.

Project details

You then have to give details about your proposed project, including: a description, its location (and ownership of the site), the sport(s) it will benefit, and the existence of any similar facilities. A further part asks for technical and safety information, and for the names of any professional advisers you have used in drawing up your project. It also expects you to show the degree to which your project will be accessible to people with various disabilities.

Project costs and funding

The next sections request information about the estimated project cost, and a breakdown of the costs and the sources of funding for the project, including the level of support needed from the Scottish Sports Council. You should also state the amount your own organisation is contributing from its own resources, and where the remainder of the money is expected to come from. The next section deals with project costs when it is up and running, and you have to give details of how day to day revenue funding will be provided.

Supporting documentation required:

- A copy of your Constitution or Memorandum and Articles of Association (not statutory authorities).
- Latest annual accounts and balance sheet.
- Evidence of ownership of project site (not statutory authorities), and a copy of any lease, draft lease, rental or access agreement.
- A copy of any feasibility study and/or design brief, along with an drawings, site plans and/or location plans.
- Full or outline planning consent.
- Schedule of equipment (if any).
- Project brief (projects costing over £100,000 only).

Use of proposed facilities

This section requests information about the current users of any facilities you may operate and of the expected users of the proposed facilities. You also have to give details of the availability of the facilities to members and to the general public, how access will be granted, and the coaching opportunities which will be offered.

Project policy

The final section deals with the ways in which your proposals fit into national, regional or local sports development strategies. You also have to state why you believe your proposed facility is needed, what you hope to achieve, how you intend to do this, and how you will measure progress.

The completed application form and supporting documentation should be sent to the address shown at the end of this section. If you need advice at any stage, you should contact the Lottery Sports Fund Unit on 0131-339 9000. Written guidance on technical matters is available in the form of a series of Technical Digests produced by the Scottish Sports Council.

ONCE YOU HAVE APPLIED

1. Receive letter of acknowledgement

You should be sent a letter of acknowledgement once the Scottish Sports Council has received your application.

2. Consultation process

The Scottish Sports Council will then assess your application, and consult with relevant bodies.

3. Decision

Decisions will be made by meetings of the Scottish Sports Council, which will take place monthly for projects with a total cost of less than £100,000 and quarterly for projects involving a larger total amount. The possible outcomes are:

- Approval of award, either full or conditional
- Carried forward to next meeting – usually only for high quality projects which might have been successful but encountered strong competition.
- Rejection of application: after which you cannot re-submit an application for two years.

CONTACT ADDRESS

Lottery Sports Fund Unit, Scottish Sports Council
Caledonia House, South Gyle
Edinburgh EH12 9DQ
Tel: 0131-339 9000 Fax: 0131-339 5361

WALES

The Sports Council for Wales administers SPORTLOT – the Lottery Sports Fund for Wales – which receives 5 per cent of the total lottery proceeds allocated to sport in the UK. At the time of writing, the Sports Council for Wales had not yet issued full application packs, available from January 23rd 1995. Applications can be submitted from the end of January 1995 (compared with January 4th for the other sports distributors). It does, however, issue an information booklet entitled *Does Your Sports Project Qualify for Lottery Funding?* which also includes an application pack request form.

ELIGIBLE BODIES

The Sports Council for Wales will only provide funding for bodies and projects which exist primarily for the benefit of a sport or group of sports recognised by the UK Sports Councils (SEE TABLE 76). Applications can only be submitted by bona fide organisations, which should be based in Wales. Your organisation will be eligible to apply if it is:

- A formally constituted club, association, voluntary body or trust.
- A governing body of sport.
- A local authority, district council or other public body.
- A school, college, university or other educational establishment (but only if there is a local identified sports deficiency and there will be substantial public access).
- A commercial organisation (but only if the project is primarily for the public good and not private profit).

EXCLUDED BODIES

The following are not eligible to apply for funding from SPORTLOT in Wales:

- Individuals seeking funds on their own behalf.
- Organisations based outside Wales.
- Bodies over which the Sports Council for Wales has material influence or control.
- Commercial organisations and professional sports clubs if their proposals are for commercial gain rather than the public good.

ELIGIBLE PROJECTS

Priority will be given by SPORTLOT for capital projects whose 'main purpose is to provide a facility which directly enables people to take part in sport or raises standards of performance'. Examples of such projects include:

- New, upgraded or extended playing facilities.
- Purchase of land, water or facilities.
- Changing accommodation for participants.
- Major sports equipment, but only if it has a permanent base and will remain in use for at least five years.
- Ancillary and support facilities which are essential for participation or performance.

The following criteria should be taken into account when considering whether your project is eligible to apply for funding from SPORTLOT:

Capital projects

Your project must involve either capital expenditure on building and construction, purchase of land or land rights, or the purchase of capital equipment. Revenue funding of day-to-day operational costs is unlikely to be provided.

Partnership funding

The Sports Council for Wales will not use lottery funds to support the entire costs of your project. Lottery funding will be provided up to the maximum limits shown below, with the remainder of project costs being met either by your own organisation (at least 10 per cent if you are a voluntary body) or by other non-lottery funders.

- *Projects of local-significance*
  Voluntary sector   70%
  Private and public sectors   50%
  Education (public and private) sectors   50%

- *Projects of regional and national-significance*
  Proportion will be determined on merit.

Minimum total project cost: £5,000

SPORTLOT funding will not normally be provided for projects with a total cost of less than £5,000.

Quality of project

Your project should be fit for its purpose, well-designed and of high quality. Any facility should also meet the minimum technical standards for the relevant sport(s).

Financial viability

Your project must be financially viable, with adequate capital and revenue funding to start, complete and sustain it.

Community benefit and support

Your project must benefit the local community and not be primarily for private gain.

SPORTS

Accessibility

Projects must be accessible to the general public for a substantial part of the time (particularly if your organisation has a restricted membership). No individual should be unreasonably denied access to your facility, and buildings must provide access for people with disabilities.

In addition to the eligibility criteria listed above, the Sports Council for Wales cites the following additional factors which will give your project a greater chance of success:

- Your project should meet an accepted sports need, either in an area or for a particular sport.
- Your project should be supported by the community and should have significant partnership funding.
- Your project should show links between schools and sports, and offer the opportunity of greater use by the wider community of schools' sports facilities.
- Opportunities should be provided school-aged children.
- Facilities should be multi-purpose or serve more than one sport.
- Your project should be part of, or contribute to, any wider schemes of development supported by your sport's governing body.
- Existing facilities should be safeguarded.
- Coaching and training – access to coaching should be demonstrated, and specialist training/playing facilities should be provided in line with wider strategies.

EXCLUDED PROJECTS

Projects with a total cost of less than £5,000

Only projects with a total cost of more than £5,000 will normally be considered for funding.

Repairs

Funding will not be provided for the repair or maintenance of existing facilities.

Personal equipment

Only major capital equipment is eligible – smaller pieces of equipment for the use of single individuals will not be funded.

Non-essential ancillary facilities

Funding will not be provided for any ancillary facilities that are neither essential to the sporting use of a facility nor an integral part of the building.

Projects located outside Wales

Any project not based in Wales is not eligible for SPORTLOT funding, and instead should apply to the appropriate national Sports Council.

Revenue projects

Revenue funding to support everyday running costs will not normally be available.

Spectator accommodation

Funding for the construction of spectator accommodation will not normally be provided, as the aims of SPORTLOT are to increase active participation in sport.

APPLICATION PROCESS

Full details of the application process were not available from the Sports Council for Wales at the time of writing, but should be available from January 23rd 1995. However, the application process is likely to take the following form:

1. Request the information booklet *Does Your Sports Project Qualify for Lottery Funding?*

The first step is to request the information booklet *Does Your Sports Project Qualify for Lottery Funding?* from the Sports Council for Wales by contacting them on 01222-397571.

2. Complete and return *Application Pack Request Form*

You should read the guidance contained in the information booklet. If you consider yourself to be eligible for funding, you should then complete and return the *Application Pack Request Form* which is contained in the booklet. This consists of questions about your organisation and your proposed project (type, location, start/finish dates, total cost, description). This request form should be returned to whichever of the following Sports Council for Wales regional offices is nearest to your project location:

SPORTLOT Fund for Wales
Sports Council for Wales
Sophia Gardens
Cardiff CF1 9SW

SPORTLOT Fund for Wales
Sports Council for Wales
10 Quay Street
Carmarthen SA31 3JT

SPORTLOT Fund for Wales
Sports Council for Wales
Deeside Leisure Centre
Chester Road West
Queensferry
Deeside CH5 1SA

SPORTS

3. Complete and return application form

When they have received your request form, the Sports Council for Wales will then send you an application form suitable for the type of project you are proposing. You should then complete and return this application form to the Sports Council for Wales.

4. Application assessment

Your application for funding will then be assessed by the Sports Council for Wales by checking it against their criteria and consulting with other bodies. A decision will then be made, and you will be informed about the outcome. Further details of the assessment process were not available at the time of writing.

CONTACT ADDRESS

SPORTLOT Fund for Wales
Sports Council for Wales
Sophia Gardens
Cardiff CF1 9SW
Tel: 01222-397571

NORTHERN IRELAND

Northern Ireland will receive just under 3 per cent of the sports portion of the National Lottery proceeds. This money is being distributed by the Sports Council for Northern Ireland, with operations headed by its lottery director, Danny O'Connor. Preliminary decisions are made by the Sports Council for Northern Ireland's Lottery Committee, which makes recommendations to the Council, which then makes the final accept/reject decisions.

ELIGIBLE BODIES

The Sports Council for Northern Ireland will only provide funding for bodies and projects which exist primarily for the benefit of sports recognised by the UK Sports Councils (SEE TABLE 76). Organisations should usually be based in Northern Ireland, and can be:

- Formally constituted clubs, associations, voluntary bodies or charitable trusts.
- Area sports associations or national governing bodies of sports.
- Local authorities, district councils or other public bodies.
- Schools, colleges, universities or other educational establishments (but only if there is a local identified sports deficiency and there will be substantial public access).
- Commercial organisations (but only if projects are primarily for the public good and not private profit).

EXCLUDED BODIES

The following are not eligible to apply for funding from the Northern Ireland lottery sports fund:

- Individuals seeking funds on their own behalf.
- Organisations based outside Northern Ireland.
- Bodies over which the Sports Council for Northern Ireland has material influence or control.
- Commercial organisations and professional sports clubs if their proposals are for commercial gain rather than the public good.

ELIGIBLE PROJECTS

The Sports Council for Northern Ireland will normally make lottery funding available for capital expenditure on the purchase, improvement, restoration, construction or creation of assets and facilities which promote participation in the sports in Northern Ireland. The money will be targeted on 'the development of high quality, safe, well designed and built facilities aimed at attracting the community to sport and holding their interest'.

SPORTS

Examples of eligible projects include:

- Construction, upgrading or extension of indoor or outdoor playing facilities. Any projects involving the improvement of facilities must be able to demonstrate a significant increase in: capacity; the level of existing users' performance; and/or the lifespan of the asset.
- Purchase of land, water or other playing facilities.
- Purchase of major, permanently-based equipment serving a single sport.
- Changing accommodation for participants, not spectators.
- Ancillary or support facilities where essential to safe participation or part of a larger project. These can include: safety equipment, equipment stores, sports officials' facilities, conditioning suites, childcare facilities, access facilities, boundary fences, landscaping, or overnight accommodation for participants.

The following basic criteria are being used by the Sports Council of Northern Ireland to assess applications:

Capital projects

As noted above, funding will normally only be available for capital projects and not to support day-to-day running costs. Revenue funding will only be provided in exceptional circumstances.

Partnership funding

You will not be able to obtain the entire costs of your project from the Council as it expects an element of funding from other sources. The higher the degree of partnership funding, the greater your likely chance of obtaining lottery funding, as this will be taken as demonstrating community support for your project. The proportion the Sports Council will provide depends upon the type and size of your project, as shown in the box.

All voluntary sector projects .... up to 70% of total project costs will be provided.

Locally significant projects
(i.e. costing under £200,000) .... up to 70% will be provided.

Projects of district significance
(i.e. costing over £200,000) .... up to 50% will be provided.

Projects of national significance
(such as facilities for high level
competition and training) .... the proportion will be set on merit.

Minimum total project cost: £5,000

The Sports Council of Northern Ireland will normally only consider applications for projects with a total value of more than £5,000. Smaller projects may be considered in exceptional circumstances, however, where funding is not available from other sources and the projects are likely to be of sustained importance to the sporting community.

Financial viability

Projects must be financially viable, especially with respect to day-to-day operational costs and sources of partnership funding.

Quality of construction and design

Projects must be of high quality construction and design, be fit for their purpose, and should meet the minimum technical standards laid down by relevant sporting bodies.

Access

No person should reasonably be denied access to any project in receipt of lottery funding.

Other criteria

The Sports Council for Northern Ireland also lists the following characteristics which a project should have if it is to be considered a priority for lottery funding. The relative importance of these criteria will vary according to the scale and type of sporting activity:

- The project should meet an accepted sports need (either in an area or for a particular sport) which has been recognised in the local/district/national strategies.
- The project should be supported by the community and should have significant partnership funding.
- The project should show links between schools and sports, and offer the opportunity of greater use by the wider community of sports facilities at schools.
- Young people should be catered for.
- More than one sport should be serviced.
- Existing facilities should be safeguarded.
- Access to coaching should be provided, and specialist training or playing facilities should be provided in line with wider strategies.

EXCLUDED PROJECTS

Revenue funding

Funding for daily running and administration costs will only be provided for a maximum of three years, for projects which are considered a high priority, which have already received lottery funding for capital costs, and which cannot get revenue funding from elsewhere.

Spectator accommodation

The aims of the Lottery Sports Fund are to increase active participation in sports and recreation. As a result, funding of spectator accommodation will be restricted to agreed locations of regional or national importance in line with the sport's performance strategy.

Outside Northern Ireland

Funding will only be provided for projects located within Northern Ireland. Sports projects based in other home countries should apply to their appropriate Sports Council.

Maintenance

All renewals, repairs and maintenance are not considered as capital expenditure, rather as a sign of past neglect.

Personal equipment

Equipment for an individual's personal use will not be funded as projects should be for the wider public benefit.

Projects with a total cost of less than £5,000

The Sports Council for Northern Ireland will not normally consider applications for projects with a total cost of less than £5,000.

APPLICATIONS PROCEDURE

1. Obtain *Information and Guidance Pack*

The first step in applying for lottery funding is to request an *Information and Guidance Pack* from the Sports Council for Northern Ireland by contacting them on 01232-382222.

2. Send *Application Request Form* at least 12 weeks before anticipated submission of application form

If, having read the *Information and Guidance Pack,* you consider yourself to be eligible for funding you should then complete the *Application Request Form* and return it to the Sports Council for Northern Ireland. This form asks for various details about your organisation, your proposed project and its funding sources.

The Council will then send you a letter of acknowledgement, along with a customised pack including an application form containing your lottery application number (which should be quoted in all future correspondence).

3. Send *Consultation Forms* to relevant bodies

The application pack contains *Consultation Forms* which you should send to all organisations relevant to your project once you have decided to apply for lottery funding. There are separate forms to send to: national governing bodies; district council or education and library board; local sports council or other relevant body. These organisations will then forward their copies of the completed consultation forms to the Sports Council for Northern Ireland, along with their comments on your project.

4. Complete and return application form *not sooner* than 12 weeks after sending your request for the form

You should then fill in the application form, either by typing or writing in black ink and block capitals. Your form should be complete in every regard, as incomplete forms will be returned to you. The main sections of the application form are summarised below.

Supporting documentation required:

- A copy of your Constitution or Memorandum and Articles of Association *(except statutory bodies)*.

- Latest annual accounts and balance sheet *(except statutory bodies)*.

- Detailed income and expenditure projections *(except statutory bodies)*.

- Letters of confirmation of project finance.

- Site plan (where applicable).

- Draft lease (where applicable).

- Schedule of equipment (where applicable).

- Project brief *(projects with total cost over £100,000 only)*.

Building projects only must also provide the following where appropriate:

- Feasibility study.

- Building drawings or A4 size sketch drawings.

Details of your organisation

The form starts with sections requesting details about your organisation, along with information about any lottery grants you have previously requested or received.

Project details

The next section asks for a description of the project, the sport it will benefit, the proposed site, its ownership and necessary planning permissions, and the proximity of similar facilities. You also have to calculate the resultant increase in sports participation, and give details of the usage of any current facilities.

Project costs and funding

The form then asks for a breakdown of the estimated total project cost, how much you require from lottery funds, and the other anticipated sources of finance. You must show that you will be able to provide for the operational costs of the facility.

SPORTS

Technical details

This section requests information about your project's compliance with technical requirements, the degree of access for people with various disabilities, and provisions for use by either sex.

Project policy

The final section asks how your proposals fit in with other strategic plans for sport. You also have to state your aims, objectives and targets, how you will achieve these, and how progress will be assessed.

The completed application form and any supporting documentation should be returned, not *sooner* than 12 weeks after sending your request for the form itself, to the address shown at the end of this section. If at any stage of the application process you have any queries you should phone the Sports Council for Northern Ireland on 01232-382222 (Monday-Friday, 2pm-5pm only).

ONCE YOU HAVE APPLIED

1. Acknowledgment of application

You will receive a letter acknowledging your application, which will identify the Lottery Officer assigned to your case (who should be your first point of contact if you have any future enquiries about your application).

2. Consultation process

The Sports Council will then evaluate your application according to the criteria laid out above, and will consult with appropriate experts, governing bodies, sports organisations or district councils.

3. Decision by Sports Council for Northern Ireland's Lottery Committee

Your lottery officer will then present the findings of this consultation process to the Sports Council for Northern Ireland's Lottery Committee, who will make a recommendation to the Sports Council as to what its decision might be. The Council then makes the final decision, which can be:

- Grant awarded.
- Grant awarded dependent upon the provision of extra information for a more detailed appraisal.
- Proposal carried forward until next meeting, but not for more than two further distribution meetings.
- Rejection – you will receive a letter informing you, where appropriate, of the reasons for failure. Any project which is rejected cannot be resubmitted within 12 months of the date of rejection.

You will be informed of the decision as soon as possible, which should usually be within six months of your full application being received, but should be quicker if you are applying for less than £100,000.

CONTACT ADDRESS

Lottery Sports Fund
Sports Council for Northern Ireland
House of Sport
Upper Malone Road
Belfast BT9 5LA
Tel: 01232-382222
Fax: 01232-682757

CROSS DISTRIBUTOR PROJECTS

For certain types of project it may be difficult to determine which of the distributing bodies to approach for funding. If you think that your project could be relevant to more than one distributor, you should decide which one has criteria covering the *main aims* of your project and apply to that body. If you are not sure, contact the relevant bodies for guidance and if necessary the distributors will discuss your case between them to determine who can best handle your application. If a distributing body receives a request which it considers to be more appropriate for a different body, it will be returned to the applicant with advice about the correct body to approach.

If you are proposing a major project which can be divided into distinct elements, each of which is relevant to different distributing bodies, you can approach different lottery distributors to fund each separate part. You should send a copy of the whole application to each distributor, making clear it is a joint application and specifying which elements each distributor is being asked to finance. You will, however, still have to obtain non-lottery sources of funding for part of the cost of your project.

The following examples cover some of the overlap situations which may arise, and how they would be resolved:

Theatres

If your project is concerned with the restoration of the fabric or interior of a historic or listed theatre you should apply to the Heritage Lottery Fund. If, however, you want to improve or modernise a venue's performance and audience facilities you should approach your national Arts Council lottery unit.

Historic Sporting Material

If you need funds for the storage, conservation or presentation of a collection of historic sporting material or equipment you should apply to the Heritage Lottery Fund, and not the Sports Councils, which aim to encourage active participation in sport.

Acquisition and display of works of art

A museum or gallery requiring lottery funding to purchase a heritage asset such as a work of art (whether new or old) for its permanent collection should approach the Heritage Lottery Fund. If, however, you want to create separately costed facilities for temporary exhibitions of modern works you should apply to your national Arts Council.

Film and photography

Applications to finance most film and photography projects should be sent to your national Arts Council. The exceptions, however, are projects involving storage or conservation of historic film or photographic archives, which fall under the remit of the Heritage Lottery Fund.

Joint arts and sports buildings

If you want to develop a building for both arts and sports use, such as a sports hall with a stage and theatre facilities, you should submit your application to the distributor most relevant to the primary purpose of the facility, and send a copy to the other body. For example, if the project will be used more often for arts than sport you should apply to the Arts Council and send a copy of your application to the Sports Council.

Commissioning new works of art

Projects involving the commissioning of new works of art for public spaces may qualify for funding from the Arts Councils. Alternatively, they may possibly be considered by the Heritage Lottery Fund if they are an integral part of a larger capital building project.

Land improvements

The Sports Councils will consider applications for land improvement or acquisition projects aimed at supporting recognised outdoor sports such as rambling, long-distance walking, mountaineering, horseriding or caving. The Heritage Lottery Fund, on the other hand, is the appropriate body for applications concerning the purchase, repair or conservation of land of scenic, geological, ecological or historical importance.

National Lottery Charities Board

The National Lottery Charities Board will *not* normally consider applications for arts, sports or heritage activities which are eligible for funding from the other distributors of lottery proceeds (the Arts and Sports Councils, the Heritage Lottery Fund, and the Millennium Commission).

Millennium Commission

The position of the Millennium Commission confuses matters slightly, as it would not normally expect to fund projects that fall within the scope of other lottery distributors but it does not rule out millennium projects within arts, sport or heritage sectors. Millennium Commission funding will only be available to arts, sport, heritage, and charitable projects that are *exceptional*, or which because of their size (over £10m) would not receive funding from other lottery distributors. In addition, it is not willing to fund applications jointly with other lottery distributing bodies.

Part 3:

OTHER INFORMATION AND ADVICE

Appendix I

PROJECT DEVELOPMENT AND BUSINESS PLANS

Large capital projects of the type generally eligible for lottery funding require careful planning and management to ensure their successful completion. If you are requesting more than £100,000 from any distributor of lottery funds you will normally be required to provide a detailed business plan and cashflow forecast. The following notes provide a brief outline of the stages through which you should progress as part of your project development and, although most relevant to building projects, can be applied with some alterations to other types of project. This information is meant for guidance only, and is no substitute for appropriate professional advice. In addition, some of the distributing bodies issue their own guidance about project development in their main application packs.

Project co-ordination

A fundamental part of the development process is setting up an effective way of managing and co-ordinating the project. It is a good idea to establish a project committee which has responsibility for drawing up the project brief and supervising the entire project development process. The committee members with the most appropriate skills should be assigned to the role of project co-ordinator, but if there is no suitable person within your organisation you should consider paying for an outside project manager. The project co-ordinator should be given authority to make day-to-day decisions on behalf of the project committee, and should be the single point of contact between your organisation and all the outside bodies involved with your project (such as lottery distributing bodies, local authorities, professional advisers, etc).

Think about what you are trying to achieve

Once an effective management structure is in place, the next step is to put together a business plan – an outline of what you want to achieve and how you plan to do it, along with estimates of how much it will cost. You should be able to do this by yourself, but you may wish to consult an accountant or other adviser. Your business plan should cover topics such as:

- What you want to achieve
- Why you want to do it
- When you will do it
- How you will do it
- How you will pay for it
- How you will measure your achievements

You will also need to address questions such as: Is your proposed facility really necessary? What is the market? Will the project be viable? How will the project affect your organisation's finances? How will the completed project be managed? You should consider whether refurbishing or improving existing facilities is preferable to starting from scratch with a new building.

Development of project brief

A project brief is a clearly defined statement which sets out the nature of your project and its main purpose, so that your design team, professional advisers, and potential funders can interpret your plans. A project brief should normally address several key topics:

- timescale – planned start and finish dates
- cost limit, if known, and running costs
- the problems with your existing facilities (if any) which make your proposals necessary, or evidence of currently unfulfilled demand
- a list of the facilities proposed, including main dimensions and estimated capacities
- a description of how the proposed facilities will be used, and the degree to which they will be flexible in use and able to meet changing demands
- general design issues including any planning constraints, and key design factors relating to structure, finishes and services
- any special requirements for particular activities
- access for people with a disability
- whether development needs to be staged or phased, and whether you need to keep existing facilities open during construction
- marketing of completed project.

You should also start thinking about sources of funding for your project's capital and revenue costs. It is vital that you keep people such as your members, neighbours and landlord (if any) up-to-date about your proposals in order to prevent the spread of ill-informed rumours.

Planning permission and other statutory consents

If your project involves changing the use of a piece of land or constructing or altering a building you will probably need *planning permission* and/or buildings regulations approval. If your project involves a building which is listed because of architectural or historic importance you will also need *listed building consent* for any alterations. You will need the advice of an architect or planner at this stage. You should normally have at least outline planning permission (permission in principle) before making any full application for lottery funding. [N.B: your local authority has the power to make you reverse any work undertaken without the necessary planning permission – this can even include demolishing any new construction in extreme circumstances.]

Selection of architects and other professional advisers

It is normally in your organisation's best interests to commission established professional advisers – such as solicitors, architects, surveyors and engineers – to handle particular aspects of the project development. Their fees will comprise a relatively small proportion of your total project costs but will be vital to its success.

You may want to use firms with which your organisation has previous experience, or companies with a track record in the particular type of project. It is normally best to ask a number of companies to tender for your business, for example you may want to run a design competition for large projects. You should also be aware of the European Procurement Regulations which affect service contracts above a certain size (see Appendix III).

Design

You must work with your professional advisers in order to achieve a high-quality design – paying particular attention to initial big decisions rather than subsequent small details. Good architecture need not cost more than bad, especially measured over the lifetime of a building. Various design questions you should take into account include:

- Will the building be fit for the purpose you intend?
- Are statutory and other requirements met?
- Are there proper access provisions for people with a disability?
- How expensive will it be to manage, maintain and run over its intended lifespan?
- How will you compromise between speed and quality of construction?
- Will the building be welcoming, safe and attractive?
- Will the building enhance its immediate surroundings?

You must then seek the approval of your members for the proposed design.

Funding

Once you have completed the design you should go about finding a builder. You will probably want to do this through a tendering process – you should ask a number of builders to submit an estimate of how much it would cost for them to complete your design. Your professional advisers will be able to suggest the best way to do this, but you should be aware of the European Procurement Regulations which affect works contracts above a certain size (see Appendix III).

When you have selected the 'most economically advantageous' tender, in terms of quality not just price, you will at last know the cost of your proposed facilities. You can then go about raising the funding for the capital and revenue elements of your project. Apart from lottery funding and your organisation's own reserves, you may also be able to obtain grants from various statutory and charitable sources (see Appendix IV).

Construction and management

Before you sign any building contract, you should ensure that you have completed all the stages outlined above and that *all the necessary capital funding is secured and ready to use*. You must have guarantees of funding before commencing construction, as few funders, and in particular lottery distributors, will be willing to bail your organisation out financially.

When funding is secured, the contract can be signed and construction can commence. If you want to visit the site during building works you should always tell the constructor first, and whilst on site you should *never* give instructions direct to the contractor but instead should get one of your professional advisers to do so. Once work gets underway you will have to pay the constructor regularly on the basis of the work done to date.

When the building work is completed, it will be inspected by the local authority to check that it is in line with the plans they approved. Your design adviser will issue a Certificate of Practical Completion to the contractor, who will hand the building over to your organisation for necessary interior work. At this stage you must make certain that your organisation has insurance for the building, its contents and its users. For a period after practical completion, you have a chance to check for any defects in the construction, which should be rectified by your contractor if caused by faulty workmanship or materials. Once any necessary work is done, you have reached final completion of the building stage.

You can then open your new facilities. Now it's time for the hard work to begin…

Appendix II

ACCESS FOR PEOPLE WITH A DISABILITY

When setting out policy directions for the distributing bodies in the areas of arts, sport, heritage and for the Millennium Fund, the Secretary of State for National Heritage specified that all lottery funded projects must have suitable access for people with disabilities. Not only does this involve physical access to these facilities, but also equality of opportunity. This section contains brief guidance on the key disability issues which should be addressed by your organisation. These notes are only intended as a brief introduction, and you should undertake more detailed consideration of these issues. You may find it useful to contact some of the organisations listed below, who may be able to offer you detailed advice.

As a bare minimum, the following disability issues should be taken into consideration:

Physical access

New and refurbished public buildings must provide access for wheelchair users to all floors, and provide facilities for people with sensory impairments, in order to comply with Building Regulations. There are be cost implications, but such expenses need not be enormous as minor changes can make significant differences to accessibility when considered sooner rather than later.

Awareness of needs

Be aware of the needs of users who may have a disability. Staff should receive on-going disability awareness training, and managers in particular should have a good working knowledge of disability issues. Even the most accessible building in terms of physical design needs effective management to ensure full access.

Information about access

Provide information about access for people with a disability in all publications as part of your marketing strategy.

Recruitment

Be aware of the possibilities for actively recruiting people with disabilities to work for your organisation, and keep employment policies under review.

Decision-making

Take steps to ensure that people with a disability can play a full part in your internal decision-making process. You should undertake consultation with people with disabilities who make use of existing or planned facilities.

The checklist shown in the box opposite can help your organisation assess the degree to which it has considered the needs of people with disabilities.

DISABILITY ACCESS CHECKLIST

	EXISTING	PROPOSED
Physical access		
Dedicated car parking spaces		
Drop-off points		
Unobstructed external routes into facility		
Level or ramped public and staff entrances, including main entrance		
Internal and external ramps, handrails and lifts meet Building Regulation standards		
Access to all levels and areas of building (public and non-public)		
Dedicated wheelchair spaces in performance seating areas		
Dedicated toilet facilities		
Box office and/or reception area of accessible height and width		
Facilities for people with sensory impairment		
Induction loop in performance areas and at box office/information desk		
Infra red enhancement in performance areas		
Visual fire alarm system		
Braille, large print and/or raised lettering used for signage		
Sign language interpretation or lipspeakers provided		
Audio description and 'touch and feel' elements provided		
Facilities to accommodate guide dogs		
Organisational policy		
On-going disability awareness training for staff		
Accessibility information published and marketed		
People with disabilities employed and actively recruited		
Decision-making process involves people with disabilities		

Sources of information and advice on disability issues

Access Committee for England 0171-250 0008

Arts Access 0171-936 3436

Centre for Accessible Environments 0171-357 8182

RADAR (Royal Association for
Disability and Rehabilitation) 0171-250 3222

Council for the Advancement of Communication with Deaf
People (CACDP) 0191-374 3607

Disability Resource Team 0171-482 5299

Equal Opportunities Commission 0161-833 9244

The ADAPT Trust 01383-623166

Disability Scotland 0131-229 8632

Disability Wales 01222-887325

ADAPT Northern Ireland 01232-664037

Equal Opportunities Commission for Northern Ireland 01232-242752

Disability Action (Northern Ireland) 01232-491011

Appendix III

EUROPEAN UNION PROCUREMENT REGULATIONS

In an attempt to ensure that a competitive market exists within the European Union, *procurement regulations* have been introduced which affect contracts issued by public sector bodies for works or services above a certain size. In order to permit international competition for these public contracts, they must be put out to public tender (by placing advertisements in appropriate European journals) so that any company in Europe can bid for the contract.

Because the National Lottery distributing bodies are defined under these rules as contracting authorities, if you receive substantial lottery funding these regulations will affect your organisation. All recipients of money from the National Lottery must comply with the procurement regulations where lottery funds contribute over half of the costs of:

- A *works* contract (i.e. construction costs) worth more than ECU 5 million (about £3.5 million).
- A *services* contract (i.e. professional fees for advisers) worth more than ECU 200,000 (about £140,000).

You can select the most suitable company on the basis of either the lowest cost, or the 'most economically advantageous tender' taking into account other longer-term factors such as design quality. These regulations have applied to public sector bodies and local authorities for some time, but now apply to all recipients of lottery proceeds above these thresholds – including charities.

Appendix IV

OTHER SOURCES OF FUNDING

With the exception of grants from the National Lottery Charities Board, one of the major conditions for lottery funding is that you obtain partnership funding from non-lottery sources. There are a variety of possible sources which may be used in order to supply the necessary joint funding:

Your organisation's own resources

The first source of partnership funding you should investigate are your organisation's own resources and reserves. Most lottery distributors expect your organisation to provide a portion of the costs as a sign of your commitment to the project. This contribution can be in the form of money, or can consist of in-kind support such as donations of materials or the value of the time and labour provided by volunteers working on the project.

Central government programmes, local authorities and other public sector agencies

Local authorities may be able to provide financial support for your projects, especially if their assistance unlocks money from other funders. Local authorities may also be able to help provide access to funds from central government schemes or statutory agencies concerned with rural and economic development or urban regeneration. Many of these programmes are restricted to certain areas of the UK or specific economic objectives, and so may not be open to your organisation. These funding sources include: City Challenge, Safer Cities Programme, Urban Development Corporations, Single Regeneration Budget, Rural Development Commissions, Welsh Office Strategic Development Scheme, Scottish Enterprise, and the International Fund for Ireland.

Funding may also be available for specific types of project from other statutory agencies, such as: English Heritage, Museums and Galleries Commission, Historic Scotland, Scottish Museums Council, Countryside Commission, Scottish Natural Heritage, Forestry Commission, and on a more local scale Training and Enterprise Councils and Local Enterprise Companies.

Europe

Funding for major developments may be available from various European Union budgets, which have a preference for designated areas of economic and/or social deprivation in urban and rural areas, and include: European Social Fund, European Regional Development Fund, and the European Investment Bank (for loans and guarantees). They generally aim to foster economic activity and improve derelict industrial land rather than develop arts, sports or heritage activities *per se*.

Charitable trusts and foundations

There are a large number of charitable trusts and foundations which may be able to provide funding for projects of a charitable nature, although the size of grants they may be able to offer varies considerably. Some distribute their support throughout the whole of the UK and to all types of recipient, whilst others focus on specific areas of the country or certain types of charitable activity. Details about many of the larger trusts and foundations are listed in published directories including the *Guide to the Major Trusts* and the *Directory of Grant-Making Trusts* (see bibliography below). If your project is in the area of art or sport, you should be aware of the Foundation for Sport and the Arts, which distributes grants of around £50m-£60m annually.

Corporate contributions and sponsorships

Most companies now have a programme of support for voluntary and non-profit organisations. Sometimes their support is in monetary forms, but they may also be willing to provide in-kind contributions of materials or products. Policies, preferences and criteria vary considerably between firms, so you should consult the appropriate directories listed below before approaching any company. Some companies may provide sponsorship for your project. If the firm is a first-time sponsor you should be able to obtain matching funding from Sportsmatch (for sports organisations, administered by the Institute of Sports Sponsorship) or the Business Sponsorship Incentive Scheme (for arts bodies, administered by the Association for Business Sponsorship of the Arts). Both are government funded schemes aimed at encouraging business sponsorship of sporting and cultural activities.

Public appeals to individuals

You may be able to raise money from the general public through appeals, or obtain funds from wealthy patrons of your organisation.

Useful publications:

The Complete Fundraising Handbook, Directory of Social Change
Central Government Grants Guide, Directory of Social Change
A Guide to the Major Trusts, Vols 1 & 2, Directory of Social Change
Directory of Grant-Making Trusts, Charities Aid Foundation
A Guide to Company Giving, Directory of Social Change
The Major Companies Guide, Directory of Social Change
Raising Money for Sport, available May 1995, Directory of Social Change
Sources of Funding for Sport, Sports Council
Search for Sports Sponsorship, Central Council of Physical Recreation
Arts Funding Guide, Directory of Social Change
Arts Sponsorship Handbook, Directory of Social Change
Capital Grants for the Arts, Arts Councils of England, Scotland, Wales and Northern Ireland

Appendix V

CONDITIONS OF GRANTS

If you are successful in obtaining lottery funds for a capital project from the arts, sport, heritage or Millennium funds, there will be a number of standard terms and conditions attached by the distributing body:

- The grant must be used for the purpose specified in your application form, and is non-transferable. The grant may have to be repaid if there is a change in purpose or ownership during or after the project.

- Lottery funds will also have to be repaid if:
  1. your organisation ceases to operate due to any reason,
  2. you fail to apply your grant for the purpose it was awarded or you fail to complete the project,
  3. you fail to comply with the conditions of the grant,
  4. your application contained information that was fraudulent, incorrect or misleading,
  5. you have acted in a fraudulent or negligent way at any time during the completion of the project.

- If there is an underspend on your project, you must return the appropriate share to the distributing body.

- If there is an overspend on your project, your grant will not be automatically increased.

- You must supply the distributing body with regular progress reports on your project's progress, monitor its success when completed, and provide the distributing body with any other information they might require.

- Depreciating assets acquired through lottery funding cannot be sold without written permission from the distributing body.

- Appreciating assets are subject to similar restrictions, with written distributing body approval needed before they may be sold (at any time), and the vendor must show that the proper market value has been received. The distributing body may insist that any such assets are transferred to another appropriate eligible body.

- If lottery-funded items are sold, or if a lottery-funded project realises a distributable profit (which should be rare given that projects should not be for private gain), a proportion from the proceeds/profits must be paid back to the distributing body. This proportion should be equivalent to the distributing body's original contribution towards the overall project cost.

- Assets acquired through lottery funding cannot be used as security for a mortgage or other loan without the prior written permission of the distributing body.

- You must ensure that your lottery funded project operates an Equal Opportunities Policy, and that the public are given full appropriate access to the facility with no person reasonably denied access.

- Where a grant is for the acquisition of a particular item or collection, the applicant must normally retain ownership of the item(s) and maintain it appropriately.

Each individual distributing body also adds its own particular terms to these standard conditions. For example, the Sports Council for England specifies that lottery grants should be brought to the attention of the public using the facility, by an acknowledgement in your publicity or a plaque on the wall.

Appendix VI

SOURCES OF INFORMATION AND ADVICE

The first source of advice to approach should normally be the distributing body you are applying to for funding. On larger projects it is also worth consulting with your local authority and any relevant statutory agencies or governing bodies. There are also a number of other sources which may be able to offer advice, depending upon the type of organisation and project, and some of these are listed below with telephone numbers.

HERITAGE

Landscape and nature conservation projects

The Countryside Commission 01242-521381
(also has regional offices across England)

English Nature 01733-340345
(also has regional offices across England)

Scottish Natural Heritage 0131-447 4784
(also has regional offices across Scotland)

Countryside Council for Wales 01248-370444

Dept of the Environment Northern Ireland
Environment Service – Countryside and Wildlife 01232-314911

The Wildlife Trusts 01522-544400

Historic Buildings, Monuments and Sites

English Heritage National Lottery Focal Point 0171-973 3265
(also has four regional teams)

Historic Scotland 0131-244 3144

Cadw 01222-465511

Dept of the Environment Northern Ireland
Environment Service – Historic Buildings and Monuments 01232-235000

Ulster Architectural Heritage Society 01232-660809

Museum and Gallery Projects

Museums & Galleries Commission (MGC) 0171-233 4200

Fund for the Preservation of Industrial and
Scientific Material (PRISM) 0171-938 8005

V&A/MGC Purchase Grant Fund 0171-938 8500

Scottish Museums Council 0131-229 7465

Council of Museums in Wales 01222-225432/228238

Northern Ireland Museums Council 01232-661023

Special Library Collections, Manuscripts and Archives

The British Library 0171-323 7111

National Library of Wales 01970-623816

National Library of Scotland 0131-226 4351

Royal Commission on Historical Manuscripts 0171-242 1198

ART

Arts Council of England 0171-333 0100

English Regional Arts Boards:

> Eastern 01223-215355
> East Midlands 01509-218292
> London 0171-240 1313
> Northern 0191-281 6334
> North West 0161-228 3062
> Southern 01962-855099
> South East 01892-515210
> South West 01392-218188
> West Midlands 0121-631 3121
> Yorks & Humberside 01924-455555

Scottish Arts Council 0131-226 6051

Arts Council of Wales 01222-394711

Arts Council of Wales Regional Offices:

North Wales 01248-353248
West Wales 01267-234248
South East Wales 01633-875075

Arts Council of Northern Ireland 01232-381591

British Film Institute 0171-255 1444

Royal Fine Art Commission
(covers England, Wales and N.Ireland) 0171-839 6537

Royal Fine Art Commission for Scotland 0131-229 1109

Crafts Council 0171-278 7700

Craftworks (Northern Ireland) 01232-236334

Royal Fine Art Commission for Scotland 0131-229 1109

Scottish Film Council 0141-334 4445

Wales Film Council 01222-578633

Northern Ireland Film Council 01232-232444

Arts Council of Wales.. 01222-394711

Association for Business Sponsorship of the Arts (ABSA) 0171-378 8143

ABSA North 01422-367860

ABSA Midlands 0121-634 4104

ABSA Scotland 0131-228 4262

ABSA Wales... 01222-221382

ABSA Northern Ireland 01232-664736

SPORTS

Sports Council (England) 0171-388 1277

English Regional Sports Councils

    East Midlands 0115-882 1887/982 2586
    Greater London and South East 0181-778 8600
    Northern 0191-384 9595
    Southern 01734-483311
    Eastern 01234-345222
    North West 0161-834 0338
    South West 01460-73491
    West Midlands 0121-456 3444
    Yorkshire and Humberside 0113-543 6443

Scottish Sports Council 0131-317 7200

Sports Council for Wales 01222-397571

Sports Council for Northern Ireland....................................... 01232-381222

Sportsmatch 0171-233 7747

Foundation for Sport and the Arts 0151 524 0235

CHARITIES

Directory of Social Change

    Publications 0171-284 4364
    Courses 0171-431 1817

Charities Aid Foundation 01732-771333

National Council for Voluntary Organisations 0171-713 6161

Charity Commission (England and Wales) 0171-210 3000

Scottish Council for Voluntary Organisations 0131-556 3882

Scottish Charities Office 0131-226 2626

Welsh Council for Voluntary Action 01222-869224

Northern Ireland Council for Voluntary Action 01232-321224

ARCHITECTURE AND DESIGN

Royal Institute of British Architects 0171-580 5533

Royal Incorporation of Architects in Scotland (RIAS) 0131-229 7545/7205

Society of Architects in Wales 01222-762215

Royal Society of Ulster Architects 01232-323760

Planning Aid for Scotland 0131-555 1565

Royal Institution of Chartered Surveyors 0171-222 7000

Royal Institution of Chartered Surveyors
(Northern Ireland Branch) 01232-322877